THE LITTLE GUIDES

OVER HAWAII

THE LITTLE GUIDES

OVER HAWAII

FOG CITY PRESS

Published by Fog City Press
814 Montgomery Street
San Francisco, CA 94133 USA
Reprinted in 2003

Chief Executive Officer: John Owen
President: Terry Newell
Publisher: Lynn Humphries
Managing Editor: Janine Flew
Coordinating Designer: Helen Perks
Editorial Coordinator: Kiren Thandi
Production Manager: Caroline Webber
Production Coordinator: James Blackman
Sales Manager: Emily Jahn
Vice President International Sales: Stuart Laurence

Project Editor: Sarah Anderson
Designer: Avril Makula

A catalog record for this book is available from
the Library of Congress, Washington, DC.

ISBN 1 875137 77 7

Color reproduction by Colourscan Co Pte Ltd
Printed by LeeFung-Asco Printers
Printed in China

A Weldon Owen Production

CONTENTS

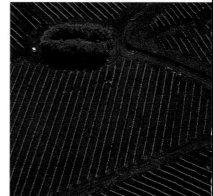

MAP OF HAWAII

On a map the islands of Hawaii look like a giant green comet shooting across the blue Pacific. The "Big Island," with its crown of fiery volcanoes, is the head of the comet. The tiny atolls far to the northwest are the thin tail.

THE ENTIRE CHAIN
Washed by storms and rarified through free-ranging weather patterns crossing the Pacific, the air in Hawaii is miraculously clear. To photographers the island atmosphere is a consummate lens. Color and focus remain sharp even at a great distances. The aerial perspective offers dramatic angles.

According to ancient legend, the air was the element of those who possessed the greatest magic: gods who could become clouds, sorcerers who released spirits to the ethers, and bird people who glided over the islands. Their knowledge came from the sky. Their flights were the pathways to a supreme consciousness. When they looked down they saw through the eyes of Uli, goddess of the heavens. For millennia the eyes of the wind have witnessed remarkable change.

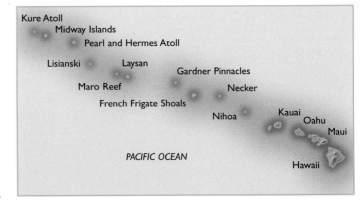

Kure Atoll
Midway Islands
Pearl and Hermes Atoll
Lisianski   Laysan
Gardner Pinnacles
Maro Reef   Necker
French Frigate Shoals
Nihoa   Kauai
Oahu
Maui
PACIFIC OCEAN
Hawaii

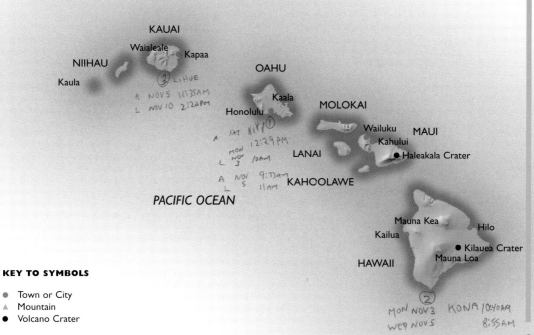

KAUAI

Waialeale   Kapaa

NIIHAU

Kaula

(3) LIHUE
A NOV 5 11:35AM
L NOV 10 2:20PM

OAHU

Kaala

Honolulu

A SAT NOV (1)
12:29 PM
MON
NOV
3   10AM
L

A NOV 9:33AM
L 5   11AM

PACIFIC OCEAN

MOLOKAI

Wailuku   MAUI
Kahului
● Haleakala Crater

LANAI

KAHOOLAWE

Mauna Kea
Kailua   Hilo

● Kilauea Crater
HAWAII   Mauna Loa

MON NOV3 (2) KONA 10:40AM
WED NOV 5   8:55AM

KEY TO SYMBOLS

● Town or City
▲ Mountain
● Volcano Crater

PART ONE

THE LAND

12

THE BIRTH
OF
HAWAII

The Hawaiian islands offer extremely diverse landscapes and climates, from snow-capped mountains and active volcanoes to tropical rain forests and pristine beaches. In length, the chain extends over 1,523 miles (2,452 km) and contains a variety of islands, including small atolls and rims of ancient volcanoes as well as the eight main inhabited islands. The Hawaiian group was formed when lava from submerged volcanoes forced its way through the Earth's crust and the ocean, to create high mountains. After an island was born it slowly moved away from the crack in the Earth's surface. Volcanic activity, erosion and movement of the islands mean that Hawaii is constantly changing.

THE BIRTH OF HAWAII

The islands of Hawaii were born in the darkness of Po, the primeval night. Here a crack of light opened. The first lava bubbled out. This was over 42 million years ago, according to geologists.

Where the crack opened, it has been determined, is where it is open still, at a hot spot on the ocean floor located 19° to 20° above the equator at a longitude of approximately 155°20'. The erupting vents at Kilauea volcano and at Loihi, the seamount destined to be the next Hawaiian island, are over the hot spot now. But they are moving, along with the entire archipelago, sliding northwest on the back of a lithospheric plate that moves 4 inches (10 cm) per year.

The Hawaiian Islands form a chain extending 1,523 miles (2,452 km) southeast to ·

northwest, near its midpoint crossing the Tropic of Cancer. There are 132 islands. Of these, 124 are minor, virtually uninhabited fragments, the rims and coral crusts of ancient volcanoes. The eight main islands—Niihau, Kauai, Oahu, Molokai, Lanai, Kahoolawe, Maui and Hawaii (the "Big Island")—feature an amazing variety of terrains for such a small area. From leeward deserts and snow-mantled mountains to sand dunes, savannahs, swamps, river valleys, rain forests, palm-lined beaches and active volcanoes, Hawaii is a phenomenon of diversity.

The islands comprise one of our youngest land forms, having arrived within the last $1/110$th of the Earth's life span of 4.6 billion (4,600 million) years; that's within the last 13 minutes on a 24-hour clock. The process that creates and destroys the chain is a slow one. An island rises out of the sea, and as it builds high into mountains, it moves. When it drifts away from the hot spot, it cools, its volcanoes die, and it is shaped by rain, wind and surf, and the plants and animals that cling to its surface.

Eventually, the island erodes away, the ocean covers it again, and it becomes a seamount. A series of such seamounts, called the Emperor Seamounts, extends northward from the top of the Hawaiian archipelago. Seventy million years ago these were

HAWAIIAN LEGEND
In legend the sea-breached crater of Lehua Island, north of Niihau, was said to be a giant crab claw that once held Hoku paa, the North Star.

islands themselves, in the same location as today's Hawaii. Colahan Seamount, thought by geologists to be the first "Hawaiian" island, lies beneath the ocean to the northwest of Kure Atoll, which is the last visible peak at the northwest end of Hawaii's undersea mountain range. The first visible peak is Mauna Kea, the highest point on the "Big Island" and the tallest mountain in the world if measured from its base 6 miles (10 km) down in the Hawaiian Deep.

The string of islets stretching away from the main islands covers nearly 1,200 miles (1,900 km). Those farthest away, including Kure Atoll, the Midways, Pearl and Hermes Atoll, Lisianski, Laysan and Maro Reef, are limestone caps resting on deeply submerged volcanic pedestals. The rest—Gardner Pinnacles, French Frigate Shoals, Necker, Nihoa and

Kaula—are the severely eroded remains of volcanic craters, none larger than a few hundred square yards. Today these windswept, nearly barren bits of land—the Northwestern Hawaiian Islands, often called the Leeward Islands—shelter fewer than a hundred human inhabitants, stationed at military installations on Kure, Midway and French Frigate. The other residents are seabirds, a few native land birds, the Hawaiian monk seal and the green sea turtle, all protected by the Hawaiian Islands National Wildlife Refuge.

The oldest main island, Niihau, lies 23 miles (37 km) northeast of Kaula and 19 miles (31 km) west of Kauai. The terrain of Niihau is dominated by 1,281-foot (397-m) Mount Paniau, the remnant of a shield volcano. The most common mountain type in the Hawaiian chain, a shield volcano is a broadly rounded peak built up by

innumerable thin lava flows. Most of the Niihau shield has eroded away, and all that is left is the cliff-truncated southwestern flank. A later series of eruptions—all low and short-lived cones—poured lava out to form the plains to the north, west and south of the original shield. In many areas this new land blanketed Pleistocene-epoch reefs that had formed 2.5 million years ago when the sea was 300 feet (93 m) lower than current levels.

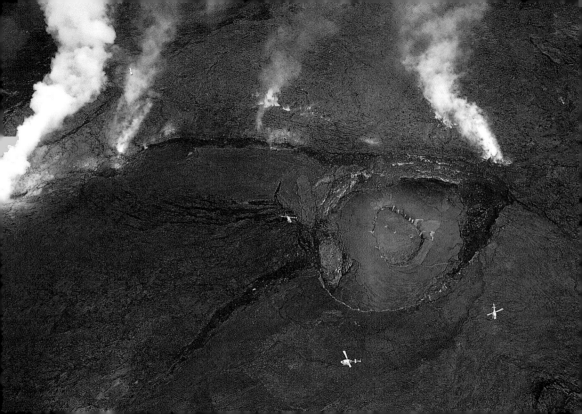

The geologic activity that shaped Niihau repeated itself on the younger islands. Typically a shield builds itself thousands of feet above the sea. Rainwater runoff wears away the peak and cuts the slopes into canyons and valleys. The surf carves sea cliffs. When enough soil has appeared, the first wind and waterborne seeds sprout. Coral polyps take hold in the shallows and begin to fringe the island with reef. With sea level changes, the ocean intermittently exposes or inundates the reefs. Then, in the final stages of the island's growth, a late volcanic series contributes primarily lowland cones that spread their lavas out in plains and capes. Alluvium from the eroding mountain washes over these flows and provides more soil for complex forests.

About 6 million years ago—after much of the original shield of Niihau had eroded but long before its plains fanned out—a single, massive shield volcano emerged to the east. The lava mountain featured a huge caldera, 10 to 12 miles (16–19 km) across, the largest in evidence in Hawaii, and it pumped out massive streams of molten rock. Eventually the southern slope of the shield collapsed, and two flak calderas opened on the east to create coastal lowlands. Such was the beginning of Kauai.

The giant caldera at the top of the Kauai shield has eroded away. The island's peak, Waialeale, was once along the eastern slopes of the caldera, but is now a wide plateau flattened by eons of rainwater. The most striking geological features on Kauai, the Na Pali Coast and Waimea Canyon ("The Grand Canyon of the Pacific"), were created by erosion, the Na Pali by a combination of

FORMING A CRATER

Cinder cones in Haleakala Crater on Maui. The crater was formed by streams which cut two deep valleys through the Maui caldera. These valleys met in the center of the mountain and created a deep hollow which was filled with lava by subsequent volcanic activity.

streams and surf, and Waimea by Waiaialeale's runoff. As millennia passed and Kauai took its lithospheric journey away from the hot spot, the rain-fed streams expanded into rivers, the longest rivers in Hawaii. Alluvium covered valley floors and plains, canyons deepened dramatically and sand dunes, coral benches, deserts, swamps and estuaries took shape.

By now another volcano had appeared 100 miles (160 km) south. Again it was a shield, which in time became the Waianae Range

of the island of Oahu. Geologic evidence indicates that the Waianae shield and the later Koolau shield were built upon the eroded stub of a still older volcano, perhaps as old as the truncated domes underlying the Leeward Islands. The Koolau volcano erupted after much of the Waianae land had eroded, and the lava flows from the new windward caldera pushed back the sea between the two mountains, forming a median plateau and banking against the Waianae slope. This volcanic doublet origin of Oahu would be repeated on younger islands in the chain.

With the formation of the two shields, a period of volcanic calm ensued in which the ocean and its reefs, over millions of years, rose 300 feet (93 m) above and later dropped 60 feet (18 m) below present levels. Further erosion hollowed spectacular canyons into the shields, and then a new flurry of eruptions—the Honolulu Volcanic Series, which occurred over hundreds of thousands of years—scattered cinder and tuff cones, like Diamond Head, around the southeastern corner of Oahu.

The two calderas atop the main shields were approximately the same size, 8 to 10 miles (13–16 km) long and 4 or 5 miles (6.5–8 km) across. Both have since eroded into shoreline valleys. The Waianae caldera was centered at the back of what is now the Waianae Valley, and the rains here sheared off a level plateau called Mount Kaala, the highest point on Oahu. The Koolau caldera was centered between Kailua and Kaneohe, two major land divisions on the windward coast.

As the ocean receded it turned Oahu's fringing reef into plains of coral pavement. Three Koolau mountain streams draining centrally and south converged in a single main stream that cut through the pavement and created a narrow canyon. In the softer, sedimentary land upstream of the coral, each of the three streams scooped out a broad, shallow valley. When the current epoch began and the sea level rose 60 feet (18 m), the canyon and the three valleys submerged. As the ocean filled in, it formed a three-armed harbor with a deep, narrow channel: Pearl Harbor.

On the leeward and windward coasts, more streams bit into the shields, producing deep, amphitheater-headed valleys with vertical walls. Plunge-pool action of waterfalls eroded the valley walls into the typical grooved or corrugated shape, none more beautifully than along the Koolau Range, where the trade winds annually dump hundreds

FOREST FIRE
Lava burns through the forest slopes of Kilauea volcano following an eruption on Hawaii in May 1990. This volcano began its present eruptive phase in January 1983.

of inches of rain. Several valley heads receded to a common point, the ridges between them gradually disappeared, and the result is a long curving cliff face like the windward Pali.

Two new twin volcanoes erupted to the southeast to create the island of Molokai. Again the western shield appeared first, but without a caldera rose only a few hundred feet. The eastern shield climbed much higher and later went through a secondary eruptive phase (like Oahu's Honolulu Volcanic Series) with its attendant smaller cones. One such cone formed the flat basaltic shield of Kalaupapa (Makanalua) Peninsula; another, Moku Hooniki Island off the eastern point. On the higher shield, a massive slump may have dropped half of the East Molokai mountain into the ocean, resulting in the cliffs of the north coast. Most geologists believe this

did not happen, however, and that it was receding valleys that caused Hawaii's most precipitous sea cliffs, the highest of which rise 2,000 to 3,600 feet (620–1,100 m).

Directly south of Molokai, the Lanai cone roared out of the sea. Its shield erupted along northeast and southwest rift zones, following the same pattern as the first Molokai volcano. The next two islands, Kahoolawe and Maui, built themselves along the same pattern. There was a time with the lower sea level when these sister volcanoes were all part of the same island. Geologists named it Maui Nui, Great Maui, and its area at 2,000 square miles (5,200 sq km) was roughly half the present size of the "Big Island." Today both Lanai and Kahoolawe languish in the arid shadow of Maui. Because its highest point is at 3,370 feet (1,045 m), Lanai pulls in some rain, but only

HOT SPOT
Puu Oo vent erupts on the side of the active Kilauea. This volcano on Hawaii is currently located over the hot spot, which never cools.

enough to cut one stream valley comparable to those on the northern islands. Kahoolawe is brown, barren and windswept now, but in earlier times its low surface supported an extensive ecosystem.

The island of Maui grew in generally the same way as Oahu and Molokai, with twin volcanoes and a connecting isthmus, and a rash of secondary eruptions that scattered cones across the older lava. Erosion scoured the West Maui caldera, leaving deep,

pinnacled valleys like Iao. On the eastern shield, Haleakala, streams cut so far in that two north- and south-heading valleys met at the center of the mountain, reducing the summit by 3,000 feet (930 m) to its present height and leaving a huge depression that ran in a single jagged line from coast to coast. Volcanic activity resumed, and these two valleys filled with lava and cinder cones to become Haleakala Crater.

While Haleakala refined its shape and drifted away from the hot spot, the Earth's magma began pumping through seven new volcanoes. The Kohala shield was the first to appear, nearly a million years ago, followed quickly by another vent, called Ninole, opening in the ocean 70 miles (113 km) south of Kohala. These two separated shields were the beginning of the island of Hawaii. Mauna Kea, destined to be the

chain's tallest peak, rose between the two, pushing its lavas over the southern flank of Kohala and possibly touching Ninole. Certainly Hualalai—the next volcano—abutted the others, and a single island half as big as today's Hawaii emerged.

Most of the bulk of the southern half came from Mauna Loa, the Long Mountain, which erupted as Ninole became extinct. Mauna Loa contains 10,000 cubic miles (41,700 km^3) of rock, making it the largest volcanic mountain on Earth. It was joined to the east by the sixth shield in the cluster, Kulani. Both Kulani and Ninole have virtually disappeared under continuing flows from Mauna Loa, whose lava has capped all but a few ridges of Ninole's old stream valleys.

The "Big Island's" seventh volcano, Kilauea, rises on Mauna Loa's southern flank. Kilauea's

ALWAYS ACTIVE
The Puu Oo vent of Kilauea volcano on the "Big Island." For as long as people have lived in Hawaii, not a single generation has passed without someone witnessing an eruption.

pumping lava as these words are being printed. The current eruptive phase began in January 1983, and by the summer of 1990 the lava flows had destroyed much of the coastal town of Kalapana and the famous black sand beach of Kaimu.

As the erupting volcanoes added girth to Hawaii, the erosive forces of rain, wind and ocean trimmed it away. Deep valleys typical of windward ranges appeared along the oldest portion of the island to the northwest. The Ice Age also

shaped the face of Hawaii, not only by changing the sea level but by creating on Mauna Kea a series of small glaciers that scoured the peak, leaving miniature moraines.

The glaciers and snow-capped summits of Hawaii are an indication of the variety of land forms found here. In these subtropical latitudes, over 2,000 miles (3,220 km) from the closest continent, the islands contain nearly every kind of geological region and provide an array of welcoming habitats. Only the heartiest and luckiest could make the serendipitous journey on their own: a few plants and animals, a seed, a nut, small fry, an occasional exhausted bird. These were the first strains in the symphony of life that would make this place one of the most unusual and fragile ecospheres known.

Hawaii stood as an impossible goal for most organisms, cushioned as it was by billions of cubic miles of turbulent water and air. Snakes never would reach its shores, nor any other reptiles (except sea turtles), nor amphibians. Land-based mammals had virtually no chance. And the odds that a nonmigratory bird could land here were one in several million. But given Hawaii's 42-million-year history it did happen (probably only once, ornithologists say) that a single gravid female finch, knocked by a storm out of her flight path and propelled into the unknown by powerful gusts, found herself in a strange new land.

By then floating seeds had sprouted along Hawaii's beaches. Fern spores had ridden in like dust on the winds. Hooked, barbed and sticky seeds arrived in the feathers of migrating ducks

AFTER AN ERUPTION
The village of Kalapana lies under this cooling lava flow. The settlement was destroyed in 1990 as a result of intense eruptions from Kilauea.

and petrels and sandpipers, plovers, tropic birds, terns and shearwaters. The birds' digestive tracts had carried in seeds of brightly colored fruits, which also sprouted. From the mud on the birds' feet had come the eggs or larvae of snails and other mollusks, and these too found amenable Hawaiian breeding grounds. Clouds nursed the plants into forests, tall, rioting, epoch-enduring rain forests that covered the old volcanoes in cloaks of green. The streams

bristled with shrimps, goby fish and snails whose marine larvae had climbed the cascades and grown into adults in the upland pools. Insects had also come, sailing through the atmosphere and alighting on the leaves. And then more birds, repeating the scenario of the finch.

The basic law of life is descent with change, and the millions of years the natural colonizers had to themselves to evolve produced startling change. From about 250 insect immigrants over 4,000 different species emerged. A single ancient pomace fly was ancestor to about 900 ornate species; one kind, *Drosophila heteroneura*, developed mallet-headed males that fight for territory like butting rams. Twenty mollusk colonizations yielded a thousand species; 250 kinds of flowering plants evolved to 1,800; 135 ferns to 168. By the

time the first Polynesians guided their canoes to Hawaii's shores, there lived here some of the most unusual flora and fauna anyone would ever see.

The birds changed too. The owl (pueo), crow (alala), goose (nene) and hawk (io) took on slightly different features from their continental ancestors, but the little finch mama proliferated at least 20 species of very distinctive honeycreepers and honeyeaters. Some, like the apapane and iiwi, developed bright red feathers that the Hawaiians used to make ornaments and capes. Other finch relatives were green and yellow: the akialoa, with long, downward-curving beak like a tendril, and the akihi-poo-laau, which sang a soft, elaborate melody through the rainforest understory.

The earliest Polynesian settlers found twice as many bird types here as the Europeans would. In

ENCROACHING LAVA
The flaming edge of a lava flow creeps through Kalapana village following a eruption from the nearby Kilauea volcano.

the ancient days a man-sized flightless goose walked the land, and a flightless rail not big enough to eat, and other flightless birds. There was a flightless owl 3 feet (90 cm) high that ran down its prey with long legs like a barn owl's. Legends tell of fierce owls that flew in flocks of thousands and of the people gathering owl eggs for food.

The only terrestrial mammal to establish itself successfully in Hawaii was the hoary bat,

a migratory native of North America. Now a unique reddish color (its mainland brothers are brown), the Hawaiian bat still lays in a reserve of body fat in late summer to prepare itself for long-distance flights. Its migratory instinct has been suppressed, however, and the fat bat sits at home.

For much of Hawaii's endemic bird population the first canoes scudding the beaches meant death. Recent discoveries of fossil bones and other remains indicate that over 50 percent of the islands' avian species disappeared after humans arrived. To make the land suitable for agriculture and aquaculture the Polynesian settlers burned off much of the lowland forests, diverted streams for irrigation, and altered the shorelines to create artificial fish ponds. In defense of the Polynesians,

it must be remembered that although their communities initially shattered the delicate sphere of natural life here, the settlers, through generations of accumulated wisdom, had become predisposed to maintaining balance in the ecosystem.

Families identified themselves with plant and animal totems. Signs in nature guided their handiwork. They labored hard for sustenance in their new home, and after more than a thousand years of practice it came easy. What they took from the islands they learned to give back. But their harmonious existence would be challenged by future settlers. And the land, which had been born as a crack of light in the dark ocean, and had been transformed by so many forces, would continue its inexorable change.

CREATING BEACHES

Black sand beaches, like this one on the Hana side of Maui, are created when hot lava hits the ocean and explodes. The particles settle as sand, and a beach forms instantly.

VOLCANOES
AND
LAVA

Hawaii is one of the few places on Earth where the land has been formed purely as a result of volcanic activity. Each island in the chain is made of at least one volcano, and some islands, such as the "Big Island," are the result of two or more volcanoes joining together. There are three active volcanoes in the island series: Kilauea, Mauna Loa and Hawaii's newest volcano, the Loihi Seamount. Hualalai and Haleakala are classified as dormant volcanoes and may well erupt again in the near future. The lava and ash that these volcanoes throw up, combined with the effects of erosion, are constantly changing the size and shape of the islands.

CONTINUALLY CHANGING

Tourists gather on the Kalapana Highway on the "Big Island" (left) to view the progress of a lava flow. The blue tarp shades civil defense officials, who have set barricades across the road. Oil in the asphalt ignites when lava hits it.

VOLCANIC RUNOFF

An anvil of iron-rich runoff on Kauai near Waimea (right), which means "reddish water."

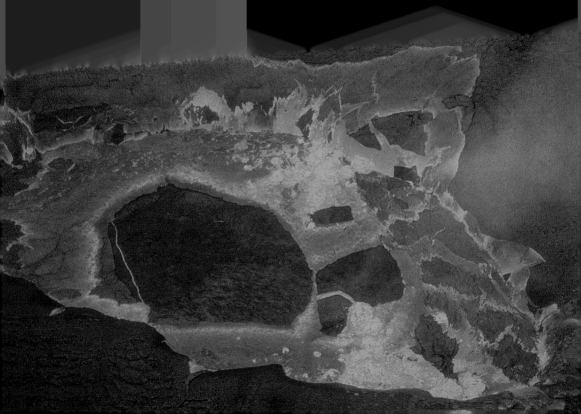

LAKE OF FIRE
A cooling lava lake near Kilauea volcano (above) cracks to reveal its red molten core.

LAVA SINK
"The blood of the Earth" scabs over in a lava sink near Kupaianaha at Kilauea volcano (left). Such depressions occur when a subterranean tube of fast-moving pahoehoe (liquid) lava burns a cooled flow above.

37

HAWAII'S HIGHEST PEAK

Like a barnacled humpback, Mauna Kea (which means "White Mountain" in Hawaiian) and its cinder cones rise above a sea of early morning clouds. This dormant volcano on the "Big Island" is the tallest peak in the Hawaiian chain; its base is 6 miles (10 km) below sea level.

BUILDING A REEF

Coral polyps attach themselves to submerged lava and begin the long process of reef building. It will take thousands of years before this baby reef along the "Big Island's" Kona coast becomes as mature and complex as Oahu's reefs.

HOT LAVA

Fiery molten lava flows (left) on the slopes of Kilauea volcano on Hawaii. Residents of nearby towns can tell how active eruptive phases are by the way the helicopter traffic increases. "It starts to look like a war zone, there are so many choppers coming in," says a geologist at Hawaii Volcanoes Observatory.

COOLING LAVA

Recent lava flows (right) at Kilauea (which means "spewing" or "much spreading" in Hawaiian) beginning to cool.

AN UNINHABITABLE ISLAND
Kahoolawe, a short-lived shield volcano that never rose high enough to attract much rain. The two points on the left, Ule Point (foreground) and Halona Point (behind), bracket Kanapou Bay in the pit of the original caldera. Lua Makika, the highest elevation, is only 1,477 feet (458 m). The island was used from 1941 to 1990 as a U.S. Navy bombing target, and much of its soil still contains unexploded shells.

EROSION AT WORK

A hot stream of dense pahoehoe (liquid) lava slid over an earlier flow of more porous aa (clinker) lava, and wave action undercut it to create this luminous tidal pond at Kiholo Bay on the island of Hawaii. Lava deltas are notoriously unstable, often areas the size of a football field will drop into the ocean without any warning.

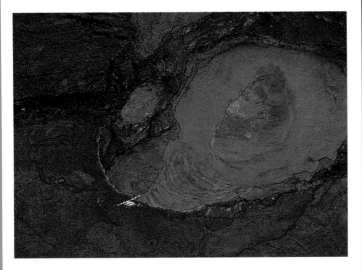

CONSTANTLY ACTIVE
Cooling lava crusts over one of Kilauea's newest pits (above). This is perhaps the most active volcano on Earth.

FIERY FOUNTAINS
Lava spurts and flares out of Kilauea volcano (right). These lava fountains, which can reach as high as 1,530 feet (460 m), characterize the explosive eruptive phases of the volcano.

KIPUKAS

Occasionally a lava flow will split and later converge (left), leaving a plot of untouched land known as a kipuka. People whose homes have been spared feel blessed by the goddess Pele.

LEGENDARY CRATERS

In the Haleakala Crater (above), the legendary demigod Maui performed two of his greatest feats: battling the Sun god, and lifting the sky. The two symmetrical cinder cones pictured here are Puu Naue (earthquake hill), left, and Ka Moa o Pele (the chicken of Pele). The cone in the center is named Halalii, after a famous trickster of Oahu or a Niihau chief whose name became synonymous with fun-making.

KILAUEA AT WORK
Lava overflows into a parking area at Aloi Crater (left) of Kilauea in the Hawaii Volcanoes National Park.

"GUSHING HILL"
The cinder cone at Puu Puai (right), which means "gushing hill" in Hawaiian. The cone was formed during the 1959 eruption of Kilauea Iki Crater.

ERUPTION ON HAWAII
Smoke and ash are expelled during an
eruption on the "Big Island." This kind
of activity is indicative of less explosive
eruptive phases of volcanoes.

EXPLOSIVE ERUPTIONS
The east vent of the Mauna Ulu rift (left) of Kilauea volcano expels molten lava during an explosive eruptive phase.

SPECTACULAR FORMATIONS
A lava bubble (right) is formed at a vent on Mauna Ulu, Kilauea Iki Crater.

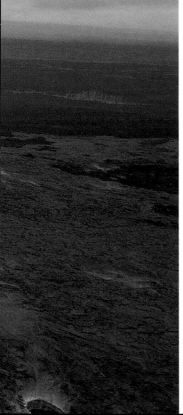

DRAMATIC EXPLOSIONS

Lava spurts and bubbles from the east vent of Mauna Ulu, Kilauea (above) and a small lava bubble forms during an eruption.

SMOKING VENTS

The smoking streams from vents and lava on the slopes of Kilauea volcano (left) during an eruption in May 1990.

INLAND HAWAII

The hinterland of the Hawaiian islands affords particularly spectacular scenery and land forms. Now-dormant volcanoes have become imposing mountains. Erosion, caused by rainwater runoff which built into rivers, has created deep valleys and dramatic canyons. Waimea Canyon on Kauai, known as "The Grand Canyon of the Pacific," was formed in just this way. The alluvium-rich valleys and plains of inland Hawaii are the breeding grounds for an immense variety of flora and fauna. The isolation of the islands has fostered the development of unique and precious species.

HOARY HEAD
Surrounded by the Koloa Basin, the Hoary Head Range of Kauai ends at a sun-flaring Nawiliwili Bay.

"HOUSE OF THE SUN"
Hunkering down into the clouds, the southwest flank of Haleakala (left), which means "House of the Sun," features a string of cinder cones that open along a fault line from the summit to the sea.

WAIMEA'S MYTHOLOGY
According to a Hawaiian proverb, "The gods build houses in the sky, and no human may visit." Much of Kauai's landmass remains untrekked, like these upper reaches of Waimea Canyon (right). Crumbling rock and flash floods discourage climbers.

DRAMATIC EROSION
Only the rains of Waialeale (above), the wettest spot on Earth, could cut so precipitous a gorge. This Na Pali stream drops 4,000 feet (1,240 m) in 2 miles (3 km).

HAWAIIAN FLORA
Ancient craters along the Pali o Kulani (right) near South Point, Hawaii. The dark green vegetation lining the bowls and hugging the cliffside is Christmas berry. The light green clusters are kukui (candlenut) trees.

POWERFUL WIND EROSION

If Waimea Canyon on Kauai is reminiscent of the Grand Canyon, then this wild landscape west of Kanepuu Forest on Lanai (above) compares with Utah's Cedar Breaks. Wind, more than water, has caused the erosion here.

VOLCANIC REMAINS

Pinnacles and bluffs, like this one in Waimea Canyon (right), are the remains of volcanic cones of dense, erosion-resistant lava.

LUSH VEGETATION
Usually shrouded in rain clouds and mist, this verdant canyon north of Waimea, Kauai (left), is just a few miles below Waialeale peak, the wettest spot on Earth.

UNSPOILT VALLEYS
Makua Valley (right), one of the last undeveloped valleys on Oahu, is a typical amphitheater-headed valley exhibiting alluvium slopes and fluted walls. In the distance Kaena Point sticks out like a bird beak.

HARDY PLANTS
Wind-combed naupaka shrubs and ironwood trees (left) adorn the coast of northeastern Lanai. Trade winds funneled through the Pailolo Channel batter the coast.

UNTOUCHED WILDERNESS?
This forest canopy on Haleakala, Maui (above) has the appearance of a pristine wilderness. But the introduced mango trees (red leaves) and hala (light green) show the impact of people.

73

THE "BIG ISLAND"

The impressive, rich valleys of Hawaii (left). This island was formed by the union of five separate volcanoes, two of which are still active today.

ANCIENT VOLCANOES

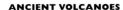

View from the Anahola mountains, on Kauai, looking south (right). The mountains were once an active volcano before Kauai drifted away from the hot spot.

"CLOUD FORESTS"
The upper elevations of several
Hawaiian islands (left) are covered
by "cloud forests," vegetation so
high that it receives moisture directly
from clouds instead of falling rain. This
cloud forest upslope of Hana, on the
eastern side of Maui, grows over a
stream-etched base of old cones and
lava flows.

IMPRESSIVE WAIMEA
Ferrous-cloaked bluffs of Waimea
Canyon (right), on Kauai.

PRIVATE ISLAND

The windblown ridges of Lanai (left). the smallest and most undeveloped of the major Hawaiian islands. The entire island was once privately owned although it is now accessible to the public.

WAIMEA'S FORESTS

Constellations of iliau (genus *Wilkesia*) spread their particular shade of green over the ridges of Waimea Canyon (right).

FERTILE VALLEY
Rain-fed Waimea River (left) bends in quiet sunlit arcs beneath the familiar pale green leaves of kukui (candlenut) trees. Hawaiians planted kukui by simply dropping the nuts wherever they wanted trees. Sometimes they hiked along ridges and tossed the nuts into ravines below.

DRAMATIC VISTA
Mist in Waimea Canyon, Kauai (right). Striking views like this attract many tourists to the canyon.

NATURE'S BEAUTY
A rainbow over Waimea Canyon, Kauai (left).

TROPICAL FORESTS
Ohia trees (right) amidst tropical forests in Halalea Forest Reserve on Kauai Island.

84

COASTAL REGIONS

The coastlines of the Hawaiian Islands include a variety of landforms and scenery—from towering cliffs and isolated black volcanic beaches to coral reefs and sheltered havens for marine life. Some parts of the chain are accessible only by boat or helicopter, while others are part of the well-worn tourist trail. The coasts and shapes of the islands are constantly changing as the sea erodes and undermines the land. Volcanic eruptions and lava flows often create new black sand beaches and lava deltas which spread into the sea. Spectacular evidence of this continuing change can be viewed in the cliffs of Na Pali and Pelekunu Valley.

INACCESSIBLE BEAUTY
Twin pinnacles (left) jut into the clouds above Na Pali (meaning "cliffs" in Hawaiian) on Kauai. These cliffs rise up to 4,000 feet (1,220 m) and are almost inaccessible except by hiking, helicopter and boat.

NA PALI CLIFFS
A rainbow forms over the southern coastal cliffs (right) of Na Pali on Kauai Island. Parts of this region can be viewed from the 11 mile (18 km) Kalalau hiking trail.

BREEDING GROUNDS
Reef fish spawn in sand pockets like this one at Onomea Bay (left) on the "Big Island."

SCULPTED BY WATER
The northern end of Na Pali (right), at Haena on Kauai. Sculpted by freshets, or sudden floods in rivers, cutting ever-expanding V-shaped valleys into the lava shield and by surf biting into the cliffs, Na Pali exhibits the grooved or "fluted" valley walls found on many high islands of the Pacific.

PELEKUNU VALLEY

Some geologists theorize that the high cliffs of Molokai's Pelekunu Valley (left) were carved by a massive earthquake that cracked the old volcano and dumped the northern half into the sea. They cite as evidence submerged debris slides reaching into the Hawaiian Deep. The prevailing theory, however, is that pounding surf undercut the cliffs, causing the upper rock to shear off.

KEE BEACH

Rugged cliffs end abruptly at the famous Kee Beach (right) located at the foot of the Na Pali walking trail on the north shore of Kauai Island.

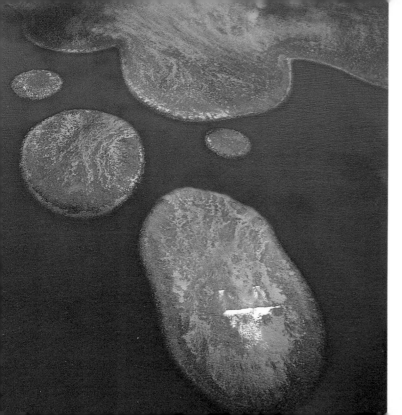

MARINE HAVEN
The reefs of Kaneohe Bay (left), just 15 miles (24 km) north of Honolulu on the windward side of Oahu. The growth of these high-rising coral heads is influenced by currents. The sheltered bay is a haven for tropical fish, sharks, turtles, rays and other marine life.

RESHAPING LEHUA
Sea caves forming on the western arm of Lehua Island (right), off Niihau. Further wave action will hollow the caves into sea arches, and then into sea stacks when the tops fall in.

"PLACE OF REFUGE"
Sunset over the Kona Coast (left)
on the western side of the "Big Island."
Puuhonua o Honaunau ("Place of
Refuge") on the Kona coast has an
abundance of marine life and is a
popular spot for diving and snorkeling.

BIRTH OF AN ISLAND
The northern plain of Niihau Island
(right) was formed by a series of
low-rise cinder cones and lava streams
that erupted after the formation of the
island's shield volcano. Lying beneath
the clouds to the left is Mount Paniau,
part of the original shield.

DUNES ON LANAI

Coastal sand dunes and grasses on the west coast of Lanai Island (left). At only 121 square miles (313 sq km), Lanai is the smallest of the major Hawaiian islands. The island is relatively arid because its mountain did not rise very high and hence it does not attract significant amounts of rainfall.

TWIN FALLS

Waterfalls on the north coast of the Kohala district on the "Big Island" (right). The effects of water erosion are dramatically displayed by the valleys carved by these rivers and waterfalls.

BLOWHOLES
Napili blowhole (left) on Maui. There
are several blowholes in the islands,
created when erosion pops the top
of a sea cave and the in-rushing waves
power mist through the opening.

KOOLAU RANGE
The southeastern spur of the
Koolau Range above Waimanalo,
on Oahu (above).

99

PART TWO

THE FIRST PEOPLE

102

THE FIRST HAWAIIANS

Archaeologists believe that the Hawaiian islands may have been inhabited for more than 2,000 years, although little is known about the aboriginal people. Historians and anthropologists have no exact information regarding the arrival of the second wave of settlers to Hawaii or exactly where they came from. The predominant theory is that these people set out from Tahiti or the Marquesas Islands around the tenth century AD and made epic journeys across the Pacific Ocean in dug-out sailing canoes to reach the Hawaiian chain. They brought with them many plants and animals, as well as a new culture.

THE FIRST HAWAIIANS

**In the myths of Hawaii man rose from the earth
and reached for the heavens. He was the striver,
rooted in the practical but aspiring to his dreams.
His body came from the gods, who created him out
of dirt, air and water, the four basic elements: dirt
for substance, air for breath, and two kinds of
water—the ocean and rain—for movement.**

Like the islands, the race called ka
poe (the people) sprang from their
earth mother, Papa, and lived
beneath the sky father, Wakea. The
water that fell as rain, the seeds of
Wakea, blessed the ground with
streams and springs and brought
forth life. Each island was a basin
that filled with the rainwater and
gave birth to wao kele (the rain
forest). Ka poe believed they too
sprang from the land, not just as
walking plants or walking earth,
but as manifestations of everything
in their world: roots, branches,

mud, rock, wind and sky, the
children of the rain forest, the
children of the volcano. Theirs
was a sexual universe in which the
mingling of all cosmic dualities—
male and female, light and dark,
high and low—were explained
in human terms. They saw the
thighs of Wakea in a cloud shape
with his rain shaft pounding the
land. They saw Papa spread her
legs in the sea and give birth to
a mountain.

Ka poe grew and prospered.
They learned to change their body

TRADITIONAL SOCIETY

The fishing village of Lapakahi on the
"Big Island," site of 1968 archaeological
diggings. Throughout Hawaii the
ancient alii (chiefs) established
wedge-shaped land divisions called
ahupuaa, which ran from coast to
mountain peaks. The people of each
ahupuaa lived in a cooperative
community, fishermen trading with
farmers and craftsmen.

into other shapes, as the clouds
and lava did. There were shark
people, eel people, bird people.
They carried their spirits into
death and back into life as
aumakua, family gods that
inhabited animal bodies and
guided their descendants. In the
ancient forests the bird aumakua
showed the people where to find

the great koa and mehamehame trees that contained canoe hulls. Ka poe cut out the hulls with basalt adzes. They wound coconut fibers into sennit cords, weaved hala leaves into sails, and set off for unknown lands beyond the horizon.

These are the legends of how the people came to find the isolated islands called Hawaii.

Scientific studies suggest that Hawaii was the farthest point in a string of islands colonized by eastward-sailing Indonesians who had ventured into the Polynesian triangle sometime before the tenth century BC. The kinds of plants and animals they brought and the similarities in language among the island cultures suggest that the groups that became dominant in Hawaii migrated from the Marquesas and Society islands. The Tahitians referred to the distant volcanic

chain to the north as Hawaiia, Burning Hawaii.

The discoverers and first settlers of Burning Hawaii sailed over the greatest body of water anyone had seen. What we know about Hawaii's aboriginal Polynesians is sketchy, but they were not the same culture that Captain Cook discovered inhabiting the islands in 1778. Ongoing archaeological research keeps pushing back the estimates for initial human contact here. The latest digs on Oahu have unearthed evidence of artificially altered landscapes and the presence of exotic pollens (of kukui, ti and taro—all plants introduced by humans) that suggest a settlement date between AD 100 and 100 BC. Common to many oral histories of Hawaii are tales of aboriginal tribes that "the first people" found already living here. These were the Mu, the Wao, the Wa and the

Menehune, described variously as forest-dwelling, banana-eating, wild, shy peoples, short or otherwise inferior races that the new colonizers wiped out through warfare and interbreeding. All that remains of their culture are stories told centuries later by the conquerors, and a few stone structures attributed to their craftsmen.

The established, more "modern" Hawaiian traditions began with the new wave of settlers who entered the archipelago around the tenth or eleventh century. They came in large, double-hulled voyaging canoes that carried whole families, and dogs, pigs, chickens, water gourds, coconuts, sweet potatoes, kukui nuts. The navigators kept star charts made of wicker and shells. They watched the fish, sharks, dolphins and whales, all aumakua, and they read the movement and colors of the sea

THE GREAT WALL

The Great Wall of Puuhonua o Honaunau which is 1,000 feet (310 m) long, 10 feet (3m) high and 17 feet (5 m) thick, was a place where fleeing enemies of angry chiefs could find sanctuary. The National Park Service administers the 180-acre (72-hectare) City of Refuge at Honaunau, Hawaii, and directs its archaeological projects. Originally the entrance to the Puuhonua (place of refuge) was only by sea.

and sky. On the stern of each hull they carved tikis with staring mother-of-pearl eyes.

Where the first of the new wave of settlers reached landfall is uncertain, although one of the ancient chants names Lanai, the small island west of Maui. Lanai means "day of conquest," possibly because it represented the dawn of conquest over the original inhabitants.

For some people, Hawaiiloa, a famous mariner and fisherman of Tahiti, was the discoverer of the Hawaiian Islands. He found the "Big Island" first and sailed home to fetch his relatives. They settled on all the islands, and many places bear their names: the volcano Hualalai after Hawaiiloa's wife, Hamakua District after their last child, the rock islets Lehua and Nihoa after men in Hawaiiloa's entourage. On one of his return visits south, Hawaiiloa discovered

his brother Ki had abandoned the family gods in favor of the man-eating god Kuwahailo (Ku of the maggot-dropping mouth). Hawaiiloa therefore made a declaration called Papaenaena (forbidden with red-hot rage) that cut communication with the Tahitian homeland, and for centuries there were no voyages between the two island groups.

Hawaiiloa is also said to have undertaken a voyage to the cold lands of the "slant-eyed" people. He brought back two members of this peculiar race to Hawaii, where the natives admired the strangers' eyes and pale skin.

Of subsequent migrations the two most notable, and those from which Hawaiian legends derive the best stories, are those of Maui and Pele.

The explorer Maui was also a fisherman. He carved a fishhook

ANCIENT TEMPLE

Mookini heiau, erected by the warrior chief Paao in the twelfth century in Kohala, Hawaii. Kamehameha the Great was born near here, at a stone called Pohakuhanaualii (stone of royal birth). The oracles had long predicted the coming of a fierce warrior who would unite the islands by force.

from the enchanted jawbone of his half-living, half-dead grandmother and pulled up islands with it. Some say he fished up the entire Hawaiian chain. Then he stood on the summit of Haleakala on the island named for him and pushed back the sky. He wrested from the alae (the sacred mud hens) the secret of which trees had fire hidden in their branches; the alae taught him how to make a fire plow, a pointed stick that he rubbed in

the groove of a dry limb until it made embers.

The Maui stories may be metaphors. A figurative way of saying Maui was a great navigator who discovered new islands: He fished them out of the sea. He expanded the horizon by lifting the sky. He learned the secrets of the forest, which plants held fire and which held various herbal remedies. His exploits earned him demigod status throughout the entire Polynesian pantheon.

The Pele myth cycle is the most extensive one recorded. Pele was born as a flame on the tongue of her mother Haumea. Pele's youngest sister, Hiiaka, emerged as an egg. Babies sprang from Haumea in strange ways, from her breasts, from her forehead.

Pele had an older sister named Namakaokahai, a jealous, merciless virago whose husband fell in love with Pele. Namaka

wanted to kill the lovers, but they escaped, along with most of the family including Pele's parents and cousins. To avoid Namaka's wrath, they had to abandon their home islands. The group sailed north in the double-hulled canoe Honuaiakea, looking for a distant group of islands they had heard of. On the voyage Pele carried the Hiiaka egg nestled between her breasts to keep it warm. Hiiaka's full name after birth became Hiiaka-i-ka-poli-o-Pele (Hiiaka in the breast of Pele). Meanwhile, Namaka's rage grew. She built her own canoe and followed the fugitives' sea path, hoping to catch Pele and exact her revenge.

Honuaiakea crossed the ocean and landed first at Nihoa in the Leeward Islands. Pele had already leaned volcano sorcery from her uncle, and she dug into Nihoa with a fire "divining rod" called Paoa, looking for lava. She struck

only water. They sailed on to Niihau and Kauai, where Pele dug again and found more water. On Oahu, Pele's clan traveled down the windward coast. They discovered a beautiful cave on a narrow northern peninsula where the waves broke over an expansive, shallow reef. One of the travelers—a woman named Kahipa who was famous for having long breasts—stayed here and made her home.

Farther down the coast at Kualoa several other members of the group, including Pele's parents Kanehoalani and Haumea, decided to settle. The rest moved on to Molokai, where Pele again dug for and failed to find the Earth's fires. On this shark-shaped island Pele's brother Kamohoalii remained. His kino lau (animal body) was a shark, and he had already become a shark many times to lead

DOORWAY TO KAPAAHEO

Waipio Valley on Hawaii. According to legend this valley contains one of the entrances to Kapaaheo. This is the place to which souls that have wandered from their sleeping bodies could be banished if they offend the gods during their travels. Kapaaheo was ruled over by the lord of the spirit world—Milu.

Honuaiakea through the unfamiliar northern waters.

From Molokai's shores Pele could see the huge volcanoes to the southeast. She headed toward them. Her quest for lava ended on the island of Maui, in Haleakala Crater. Here she opened cinder cones and spatter cones and lava rivers, and she shot the molten rock into fountains so high they lit up the night like rising suns.

By now Namaka had sailed within range of Hawaii, and when she saw the volcanic celebration firing up the sky she knew where Pele was. She caught Pele on the Hana slope and killed her, burned her body and scattered her bones over the land. Pele's magic was so powerful, however, that she was able to restore herself. Her apotheosis came at Mauna Loa on the "Big Island," where her spirit collected all the bodies a woman grows through, from young girl to haggard crone. People would see the goddess after this—and still do see her—in many of her manifestations. Usually her appearance exemplifies goddess: mature, radiant, sexually desirable. Sometimes she comes as an old woman with snow-white hair, often walking a snow-white dog. Sometimes she is glimpsed in the smoke rising from the volcano, or in the fire fountains and shifting lava.

Pele's power has fired the volcanoes of the Big Island almost unceasingly since the Hawaiians settled here. Her destruction and construction of the landscape are the source of many tales, including contemporary stories about the eruption she started in 1983, said to be an angry reaction to the geothermal drilling in the Puna District.

The impact of Pele in Hawaii extends beyond vulcanism. She is

AN HAWAIIAN STAPLE
These dry-land taro plots above Waimea on Kauai are laid out in the shape of the haloa (long root stalk) of the taro. This was one of the staple food stuffs of the first Hawaiians. It is believed the vegetable is not indigenous but arrived with the human immigrants.

credited with the wide dispersal throughout the islands of the hala, or pu hala (pandanus or screw pine) trees. It happened that when she landed her canoe on the shore of the "Big Island" it got entangled in the aerial roots of the hala. Pele had so much trouble extricating her outrigger that she started tearing apart the trees and flinging bits all over. They landed on every island and sprouted.

The ulu (breadfruit) tree also spread in a legendary fashion. The first ulu were the oversized testicles of a man in the islands whose relatives cut them off somehow, cooked them in an earth oven and had their friends over for the feast. When the friends discovered they had eaten testicles they vomited everywhere for days, propagating the breadfruit.

In fact, the early settlers brought the ulu with them in their canoes. Each double-hulled waa carried 20 to 40 people, along with the agricultural seedlings and transportable food stuffs the voyagers needed to survive. They brought the plants favored by their Indo-Malayan ancestors: yams, taro, gourds, ti, sugarcane, bananas, bamboo, mountain apple, coconut, sweet potato, paper mulberry, hibiscus, wild ginger, turmeric, kukui and hala. Animals shared the crowded canoe space as well—those pigs, chickens and dogs the Hawaiians packed in cages, and the rats and insects that rode as stowaways.

As more people landed on Hawaii's shores and the established families grew, there began fierce competition for land. Raids escalated into border wars. However, there were times of peace as well when the chiefs, called alii, had the mana (spirit power) to establish just laws. They saw how dangerous their increasing population was to the forest and the fish habitats, and they expanded their system of kapu to include conservation. Overcultivated and overfished areas became forbidden, kapu, until the alii declared them abundant again. Then the makaainana (commoners) could harvest freely.

The alii governed with the guidance and consent of the priests. Kapu could not be enforced without the threat of supernatural punishment. Four great gods, called akua, ruled the world: Kane, the god of sunlight, water and forests, the god of creation; Kanaloa, the god of the ocean; Ku, the god of war and other work by men; and Lono, the god of harvests. The gods watched over the islands from the clouds, and the kahuna (priests) listened to their voices on the wind. Religion controlled every kind of behavior; in fact, it so permeated

A WATER GOD

In legend, the demigod Kamapuau watches over Hawaii by maintaining the water supply and protecting the abundance of the land. Once the lover of Pele, Kamapuau now roams the waterfalls of the islands.

the culture that the Hawaiian language had no separate word for religion. Temples were built. These were rock platforms and walls with tikis (in Hawaiian, kii) standing guard over the altars and sacred huts. In oracle towers the kahuna stood closer to the sky. With air above them and air below, the priests were in the element of divinity. They understood the currents of the sky the way navigators understood ocean currents. The temple was called a heiau: *hei* meaning to ensnare, *au* the energy of the sky.

In the twelfth century a new priest named Paao migrated from Tahiti, bringing sterner laws. His akua was Ku, the war god. Paao built a temple for Ku in Puna at Pulama, and introduced human sacrifice. This luakini heiau (temple of human sacrifice) was called Wahaula (red mouth), for the blood. Paao quickly became a mighty warrior chief on the "Big Island," and his second temple, the heiau of Mookini at Puuepa in Kohala, is a monument to his power. A line of workers passed stones from the coast to the temple site.

Having established his preeminence on Hawaii, Paao sailed to Tahiti to bring back a cousin of the purest alii blood to help him rule. His chant to his cousin must be like other chants sung by returning Hawaiians who hoped to lure their relatives to the new islands:

Here are the canoes, come
    aboard.
Return and dwell on
    green-backed Hawaii,
A land discovered in
    the ocean,
Risen up out of the waves
From the fiery depths of
    the sea,

THE KING'S ROAD
The famous Alaloa, or King's Road, crosses over a lava flow on Maui. Constructed over 400 years ago, the road is still in good condition.

A piece of white coral left
    dry in the ocean,
Caught by the hook of the
    fisherman...
When the canoes land,
    come aboard.
Sail away and possess
Hawaii, a land.
A land is Hawaii.
A land is Hawaii for
    Lonokaeho to dwell in.

Lonokaeho, the invited cousin, declined, but another named Pili accepted and returned with Paao

to solidify the Tahitian presence in green-backed Hawaii. Under Paao the Ku ritual and priesthood spawned a succession of kahuna that ran unbroken through 28 generations to Hewahewa, the high priest of Kamehameha the Great.

Those two pale Asians that "the discoverer" Hawaiiloa brought back in the early days were precursors. Sometime between the thirteenth and sixteenth centuries (the oral accounts are difficult to date) a storm-blown boatload of what were probably lost Japanese traders washed ashore in Hawaii—probably Japanese because they had with them a long sword that seemed made out of sunlight and that was sharper than the wind-honed ice of Mauna Kea. Possibly a samurai sword, it became a prized weapon among the chiefs. The stranded foreigners stayed and were

absorbed into the race. What happened to the sword, after generations of passing from one hand to another, is a mystery.

Spanish galleons bound for Manila next touched the islands, possibly as early as the late 1500s. Their Hawaiian discoveries went unreported in the West, and only recently have scholars posited from old charts that Spaniards were the Leif Erikssons of this new world. Whether they actually landed in Hawaii is questionable, although Cook's men were convinced the iron utensils they saw on Kauai—including skewer-like iron daggers and a broken sword—were of Spanish origin.

For the most part, however, Hawaiians developed their culture in isolation. Theirs was a unique society that to this day has never been wholly understood or appreciated by the outside world. As a race the islanders lived like

ARCHAEOLOGICAL DISCOVERIES
Ka Lae (the point), the southernmost tip of the "Big Island" and the southernmost point of land in the United States. For decades archaeologists believed the South Point area contained the oldest evidence of human habitation in Hawaii, dating back to AD 750. Recent findings on Oahu, however, predate the South Point remains by at least 600 years.

the birds of the high rain forest: virtually disease-free, happy and certain in their daily pursuits and nurtured by a fragile environment over which they held a specialized mastery.

In the late eighteenth century their culture reached its zenith. It was Paleolithic, but so advanced were its craftsmen that every human need was met with artistic flourish. Food platters,

pollen-stuffed woven pillows, tattoos, feather garments; boar tusk, whale ivory, and seashell jewelry; lime-bleached hairdos; stone mirrors, cowrie shell octopus lures, shark tooth daggers, carved spears of every wood; tikis, surfboards, musical instruments, tiny bows and arrows for shooting rats; ti-leaf rain capes, hala sandals, tapa cloth of pounded and stamped wauke bark, ieie baskets, mahiole helmets—every item and fashion had a singular and blessed existence.

The Hawaiians built terraces to grow their taro; they built smooth-faced walls and platforms of fitted stone inside shallow caves; they built rock house-platforms topped by houses thatched with pili grass; they built fortresses to guard their lands; they buried their exalted chiefs in wicker baskets and black tapa; they pecked petroglyphs in smooth lava rock; they erected shrines and altars for hundreds of gods; they found beds of dense basalt on the volcano slopes and turned them into adze-blade quarries; they danced hula and composed chants and were possessed of the most remarkable stories of any people, what the folklorist Nathaniel B. Emerson called "the unwritten literature" of Hawaii.

In the late eighteenth century Hawaiian society must have seemed nearly perfect yet it was undercut by the seeds of revolution (not unlike the high point of any other human culture at any other time). It was at this time that the people living along the leeward coasts of Oahu and Kauai gathered together because someone had spotted something, they gazed at two strange objects moving across the water—the ships of Captain Cook.

HAWAIIAN CANOE

An outrigger, or single-hulled, canoe paddling team trains in the smooth, aquamarine shallows of a reef near Kona, Hawaii.

HAWAIIAN CULTURE

The culture of the first Hawaiians was complex and sophisticated. It was a feudal society in which the people were divided into several castes. Religion had a key place and impacted on all facets of daily life. There were kapu (strict rules) relating to most activities including crop planting, fishing, family life and relations between the sexes. The people were proficient craftspeople who built stone heiaus (temples) in which to worship their gods. The first Hawaiians were navigators of great skill. They built innovative double-hulled sailing canoes in which they traveled thousands of miles across the open ocean between the islands of the vast Pacific.

HAWAIIAN TOMB

In 1650, Chief Keawe constructed this house (left) to store the bone bundles of dead alii (chiefs) at Puuhonua (place of refuge) on the "Big Island."

COASTAL CASCADE

A cascade stairway on the Hana coast of Maui (right). There are literally thousands of waterfalls in this district, fed by the abundant rainfall across Haleakala's upper slopes. Because of the water, Hana was prized as a settlement area by ancient chiefs. The Hawaiian word for wealth is waiwai (water water).

A TIMELESS PASTIME

A fisherman, wearing reef shoes and a bait bucket around his neck, looks up to see what might be scaring away his fish. This reef lies 100 yards (91 m) off the beach at Diamond Head.

ANCIENT WALLS

Remains of rock walls and platforms near Mamalu Bay, Maui (left). The masons of ancient Hawaii, using no mortar of any kind, built structures of remarkable precision and durability.

OUTRIGGER CANOE

A single-hulled canoe in the waters off Waikiki Beach (right). The ancient Hawaiians used similar craft for fishing and traveling between the closer islands. The Hawaiians could make a canoe hull out of a single piece of the giant koa tree. The building of a canoe was a long, involved task surrounding which where were many kapus. A kahuna (priest) was involved in the process—he checked the auspices and chose the tree.

PLACES OF WORSHIP
The remains of heiaus (temples) on Maui (left). Heiaus were places where the Hawaiians worshiped their many gods, although each individual heiau may have been dedicated to a specific god.

LAND'S END
Like the barbed tip of a warrior's spear, Kaena, Oahu (right), points toward the heart of Kauai, a hundred miles away. For ancient Hawaiians, Kaena was a leina-a-ka-uhane, a land's end where the souls of the dead leaped into the spirit world.

131

"THE ROOT OF LIFE"

In Hawaiian legend, Wakea's (the Sky Father) first son, Haloa-naka, died at birth and was buried, and his body became a taro plant. Ka poe (the people) are descended from Wakea's second son, also called Haloa. Thus the human race, descended from the younger son, is genealogically inferior to taro. The second sibling was to respect and look after his older brother and in return Haloa-naka, "the root of life," would sustain the descendants of the younger brother.

WHERE LAVA MEETS THE SEA

Black lava meets the sun-burnished Pacific near Halepe on the "Big Island" (right). These flows, ranging in age from a hundred to several hundred years, are too young to support much vegetation.

ROYAL BIRTH PLACE

Puuomahuka heiau in the hills above Waimea stream and bay on Oahu's north shore (left). Credited to Menehune builders, and a birthing site for royalty, this is probably the place where three of Captain George Vancouver's crewmen were offered in sacrifice in 1794.

WALLED HEIAU

A heiau on Maui (right). There were two main styles of heiau built by the Hawaiians—an older, platform type of heiau and a walled type (pictured here). This second type of heiau is associated with the stricter religious code and human sacrifice introduced by the Tahitian priest Paao in about the twelfth century.

PIILANI'S TEMPLE

The remains of the rock walls of Piilanihale heiau, near Hana, Maui (in the centre right of the image), represent the largest preserved ancient temple in the islands. The heiau was erected by Maui's high chief Piilani in the fifteenth century. A caretaker's house sits nearby.

THE FIN OF MOLOKAI

Kalaupapa Peninsula, the fin of the shark-shaped island of Molokai (left). The crater is Kauhako, whose flows created the peninsula.

HAWAIIAN AGRICULTURE

This rock enclosure on the parched southern flank of Haleakala (right) was probably an agricultural plot that was abandoned several centuries ago.

HALLOWED REFUGE

A platform heiau inside the famous Puuhonua o Honaunau (Place of Refuge) in South Kona on Hawaii. Almost every district had a puuhonua which was chosen by the chief. These areas were sacred places which protected any who entered their confines. They were surrounded by carved wooden statues, or kii's, which watched over a Puuhonua and enforced the Kapu.

KAMEHAMEHA THE GREAT
Remains of a building near the birth place of Kamehameha on the "Big Island" (above). Legend maintains that Kamehameha was born under a streaking red star named Kokoiki. This fierce warrior united the islands and became king of Hawaii in the early 1800s.

A HOLY PLACE
The ruins of a temple at South Cape, Hawaii (right). At these sacred places the Hawaiians made sacrifices or offerings to their gods. Access to the sacred temples was regulated by strict kapu laws.

KAMEHAMEHA'S TEMPLE

Puukohola (hill of the humpback), the most famous restored heiau in the islands (left). This was the temple Kamehameha built at Kawaihae, Hawaii, for his feathered war god Kukailimoku (Ku devourer of islands), and the place where Kamehameha's rival Keoua was sacrificed.

TERRACED MOUNTAINS

Nualolo Valley (right), the uninhabited "Valley of the Lost Tribe" on the Na Pali Coast of Kauai. The remains of terracing and a heiau indicate an active settlement, but the Polynesians who lived here disappeared inexplicably, possibly as long as 800 to 1,000 years ago.

AN ANCIENT ROAD
"Long Road" (Alaloa), which, unlike those on other islands, made a complete circle around Maui. Over 400 years ago, Chief Kiha-a-Piilani directed the construction of this stone path, often called King's Road.

ABUNDANT MARINE LIFE

Fishermen's platforms and ladders near South Point. The incredibly clear, deep water along the "Big Island's" southern shore teems with ulua, a species of crevalle or jack fish that grows to 5 feet (1.5 m) and 100 pounds (45 kg). Prized varieties are the ulua-aukea (red ulua), the largest; ulua-ele ele (black ulua); and ulua-paopao (yellow and green with vertical green bands), a favorite fish for eating raw.

MYTHS
AND
LEGENDS

Ancient Hawaiian society was non-literate. The Hawaiians recorded their history and beliefs in stories, songs, legends and myths. The stories were retold through mele oli, spoken or sung chants, or mele hula, chants accompanied by music and dance. Some Hawaiian myths, as found in the Kumulipo creation chant, tell of the beginning of the world; other legends relate the complicated lives of the gods; and many stories describe the origins and arrival of ka poe (the people) in Hawaii. The best-known legends come from the numerous song-poems of the Pele and Hiiaka cycle which relate the story of the arrival of the volcano goddess in Hawaii and her subsequent adventures.

DIVINE HALEAKALA

Haleakala means "House of the Sun."
Hawaiian legend reports that the
crater was the resting place of the
Sun. It was here that Maui battled with
the Sun god to make the days longer.
Here also, Pele first discovered lava in
her search for a new home.

THE LEGEND OF WAIPIO
According to Hawaiian legend, Waipio Valley (left) was slapped flat by the tail of a great fish. It was probably a tidal wave that gave rise to the myth. Waipio frequently endures tsunamis, which have struck twice within the last 60 years alone. Waipio is the southernmost of a windward row of six amphitheater-like valleys cutting their way into the "Big Island's" oldest volcano, Kohala.

PELE'S HOME
The volcano goddess Pele made her homes in firepits similar to this one. Her favorite is Halemaumau (house of the maumau fern), an older pit at Kilauea volcano (right) that had overgrown with ferns until she rekindled its fires and burned everything away.

ANCIENT MAUI NUI

From above Haleakala looking west across Maui's isthmus and south shore. The straight line cutting through the sun glare beneath the clouds is the seawall of Kealia Pond. Sections of four volcanoes of the ancient mega-island Maui Nui are visible in this shot (clockwise from top): Kahoolawe, Lanai, West Maui and Haleakala.

BLESSED BY A RAINBOW
Anuenue, the rainbow goddess, blesses Waimea Canyon (left).

THE DEMIGOD MAUI
A river of clouds tumbles over Kalapawili Ridge and pours into Haleakala Crater (right). The demigod Maui is said to have climbed to the uppermost ridges of the great volcano and there performed the feat of pushing the sky away from the Earth.

LEGENDARY MAUI

Moku Mana seabird sanctuary near Meanae, Maui. Legends about the exploits of Maui, the island's namesake, are numerous. It is told that he fished the Hawaiian islands out of the sea.

THE WATCH TOWER

Looking over Manana Island to Makapuu Point, Oahu (left), which the goddess Pele's sister Hiiaka praised in a chant: "We love the place, the watch tower, from which we can see the canoes, with their jibbing triangular sails, sailing back and forth between here and Molokai."

PELE'S FISH POND

Nomilu fish pond, Koloa District, Kauai (right). Said to have been dug by Pele in her continuing search for lava, this crater of brackish water became a sacred fish pond guarded by two supernatural eels: Puhi-pakapaka (scaly eel) and Puhi-ula (red eel). The lair of Puhi-ula is that crescent of red water up the coast. When there is an eruption in Pele's home on the "Big Island," these ponds smell of sulfur.

SUPERNATURAL FORESTS

Waihee Valley, West Maui Mountains (left). The remote elevations in the islands were called wao akua (wild forests of the gods). Supernatural influences found their source in these cloud forests, as did all life. The water from the sky fell to the mountains, the water from the mountains fell to the streams, and the streams filled the irrigation ditches for taro, the Hawaiian staple food.

THE MYTH OF MOKOLII

In Hawaiian legend Mokolii Island, off Kualoa Point, Oahu (right), is the fluke of a giant moo (dragon-lizard) that Pele's sister Hiiaka killed and chopped to bits. Today Mokolii is sometimes called Chinaman's Hat, but neither the Chinese nor the Hawaiians appreciate the name.

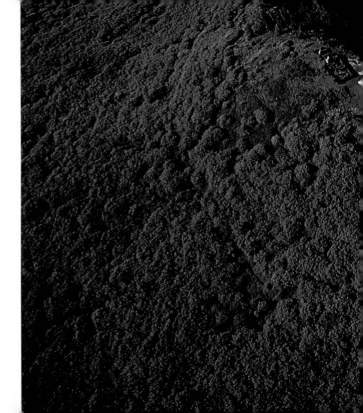

KAUHAKO CRATER

A small brackish pool inside the Kauhako crater is where the volcano goddess Pele first dug looking for lava on Molokai. After striking water she went on to Maui.

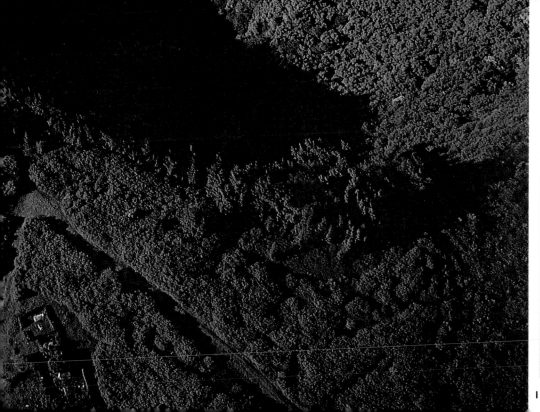

WESTERN CONTACT

THE HISTORY
OF
WESTERN CONTACT

The first recorded meeting between Westerners and Hawaiian people was in 1778 when Captain James Cook and his crew reached the islands. The arrival of Europeans was a cataclysmic event for the Hawaiians. The population was devastated by the diseases that were introduced by the Western visitors, against which the islanders had no immunity. During the nineteenth century Western immigration and influence increased, and the local culture and religion were significantly altered. At this time the islands were united as a sovereign nation ruled by a succession of Hawaiian monarchs. However, by the end of the century the Hawaiian people had lost political and economic control of their land.

THE HISTORY OF WESTERN CONTACT

It happened one rainy season, in a year their grandchildren would learn to call by a number—1778—that the people of the northernmost main islands saw something floating offshore, something odd like "trees moving on the sea."

On January 18 that year the trade winds blew in the future in the shape of Captain James Cook and his ships the *Discovery* and the *Resolution*. They sailed within view of the island of Oahu. Weather conditions forced the British vessels into a heading off Kauai and Niihau and finally back to Kauai before they could reach landfall at Waimea two days later.

It was the season of Makahiki in the islands, the period of harvest, games and relaxation. During Makahiki the people raised the standard of Lono, a billowing white tapa cloth hoisted on a tall pole and kept in the most sacred section of the heiau dedicated to the god. When the Hawaiians sighted the strange objects on the horizon they were frightened at first: "trees moving on the sea." But as the vessels came closer they seemed more like floating islands pushed by multiple cloudlike sails, then like marvelous outrigger-less canoes. The crews, they discovered, were brightly dressed white men (haoles) who carried exploding sticks and traded with beads and iron. A kahuna saw the sails as the standards of Lono and

THE COLONY AT KALAUPAPA
Kalaupapa settlement, Molokai. The dirt road leads to Kalawao, the original town for lepers on the peninsula. In 1888 the exiles abandoned Kalawao and moved here to the drier, less windy Kalaupapa side. Sulfone drugs arrested the disease in the 1940s.

announced that Lono's blessing attended these voyages.

Captain Cook named this group of islands after the Earl of Sandwich, a sponsor of his expedition. There were resemblances in body type and language between the Hawaiians and the islanders of Tahiti, New Zealand and the Easter Islands, and Cook declared these peoples one far-flung race. He wrote in his

journal, "How do we account for this nation spreading itself so far over this vast ocean?" Cook's first visit was brief. He left Kauai and headed for the northwestern coast of America. When winter set in, the Great Navigator returned to the Sandwich Islands. His ships appeared off windward Maui in November 1778. After two months of trading offshore and taking a difficult tack down the Hamakua coast of the island of Hawaii, Cook sailed around South Point and northward into the only safe anchorage he could find, at Kealakekua Bay.

The people were gathered again for Makahiki. A small fleet of double-hulled canoes carrying the chiefs, escorted by hundreds of smaller outriggers and thousands of swimming natives, greeted Cook, calling him "Rono" (Lono). From this point the story of what happened to Captain Cook has

been exaggerated. Because the Hawaiians called the haole captain "Rono" it has been assumed they thought he was their god Lono or a manifestation of the earlier chief Lonoikamakahiki, who promoted the Makahiki festival, and that they worshiped Cook as a god. But according to artist–historian Herb Kawainui Kane, "the myth of Cook as a Hawaiian god originated not in Hawaii but in Britain several years after Cook's death, when the official account of the voyage was published." British writers, creating a role model for future generations, made Cook into a classical hero complete with a death caused by hubris: Cook's pride led him to believe he was a god, so he was struck down. Hawaiians called him "Rono" only because he commanded such advanced technology that they received him as a chief of the Lono class. Their gods, as they informed

the British at Kealakekua, were invisible and lived in the clouds.

The white visitors spent several days in the bay, filling their stores with fresh water and food in exchange for trinkets and iron—"two pigs for one nail"—then they set sail for the Arctic. But foul weather and a broken mast forced them back to Kealakekua. That evening one of the cutters of the *Discovery* was stolen. Cook and 10 marines went ashore the next morning to retrieve it, and they tried to take high chief Kalaniopuu hostage. The chief's warriors moved in. One aimed a dagger at Cook, who fired both barrels of his gun. His men began shooting. In the melee, someone clubbed the captain with a fencepost; someone else stabbed him. The warriors killed Cook and four of his men, stabbing the captain repeatedly. Of the Hawaiians, four chiefs and 13

FIELDS OF TARO
The traditional Hawaiian staple foodstuff, taro, has been planted in the Western style at Hanelei on Kauai.

commoners died. The English sailors retreated.

Among the warriors involved in the attack was Kalaniopuu's nephew, Kamehameha. This young chief wanted to rule the "Big Island" and possibly Maui. He had spent many hours on Cook's ships and learned there the mighty magic of iron and cannons and gunpowder. His destiny as a conqueror became clear.

Four years after Cook's ships sailed away from the hostile islanders, Kalaniopuu died, and Kamehameha became entangled in a land war on the "Big Island" with his cousin Keoua. Their bloody battles led to a standoff. An unsettled peace was declared. By this time Kahekili, the ruler of Maui, had conquered the islands of Oahu and Molokai and married into the family of the high chief of Kauai and Niihau, securing his rule over all the islands except Hawaii.

The winter of 1789–90 brought the American vessels *Columbia* and *Lady Washington*. The latter supplied several chiefs with guns and ammunition. Later in 1790 a chief of the "Big Island" seized the schooner *Fair American*, equipped with muskets and two field cannons. He gave the prize to Kamehameha. One officer from the *Fair American* and one from its sister ship the *Eleanora* were taken prisoner. John Young and Isaac Davis became Kamehameha's advisers.

Kamehameha sailed with his men to Maui first, and while they fought toward the decisive battle in Iao (where the valley stream turned red with blood), Kamehameha's districts were being attacked and ravaged by Keoua back home on the "Big Island." Kamehameha returned and drove

JAPANESE PAGODA

The three-tiered pagoda overlooking Honolulu Memorial Park is an enlarged replica of one of Japan's architectural treasures, the Minami Hokko-ji, built near Nara during the Momoyama Period (1574–1602). Beneath its copper spire and lichen-stained roofs is a columbarium with 1,750 niches for urns bearing ashes of the dead. The nearby haka monuments will someday cover the lawns.

Keoua south. When a rare explosive eruption of Kilauea killed many of Keoua's retreating warriors, he lost heart, thinking that Pele and the other gods opposed him.

Meanwhile, with Kamehameha driving against Keoua, the enemy armies of Kahekili from Maui, Molokai and Oahu, and those of Kaeo from Kauai, combined and

attacked Kamehameha's strongholds in north Hawaii. Kamehameha assembled all his double-hulled canoes and the *Fair American* and set out to confront the invading forces. They met in a sea battle off the shore of Waimanu. Cannons blasted from both sides, but Kamehameha's superior firepower won.

On the northwest coast of Hawaii, Kamehameha had built a huge heiau to honor his war god. He invited Keoua for the dedication ceremony. Keoua went, undoubtedly knowing his fate. He and his men were killed and sacrificed on the heiau altars. Kamehameha finally ruled the "Big Island."

With the 1792 arrival of Captain George Vancouver and his undaunted preachings of peace, Kamehameha acquired the wisdom and skills of a king and declared a truce that lasted four years. He asked for the protection of the British. Vancouver agreed, in exchange for the cession of the island of Hawaii. England never accepted the agreement, but it led to British influence in the islands for many years.

After Vancouver departed, Kamehameha continued collecting islands, beginning with the complete conquest of Maui, Molokai, Lanai and Oahu. Kauai was still out of reach. Between 1796 and 1809 Kamehameha built three fleets of battle canoes and sailing ships. He was stopped first by foul weather, then by a pestilence. War on Kauai would be difficult. In 1810, long after the death of Kaeo, his son Kaumualii, knowing the power of Kamehameha's third fleet, accepted a treaty, and Kauai joined the kingdom.

During Kamehameha's reign, many countries sent explorers and

HARVEST TIME
Harvesting sorghum outside Paia, Maui. Sorghum is used in Hawaii as feed for dairy cows and other livestock.

settlers to the islands, and the fur trade between the Pacific Northwest and China brought in hundreds of "stopover" ships. Kamehameha welcomed those he judged beneficial and banished all others. The British successfully settled here, but the Russians, when they started building stone fortresses on Oahu and Kauai, were asked to go. They left behind their forts as reminders of the ongoing threat of foreign military power in Hawaii. The French arrived and baptized Kalanimoku, one of Kamehameha's chiefs, into the Christian faith. But Kalanimoku

never appreciated the haole religion and continued to obey kapu.

On May 8, 1819, Kamehameha the Great died. His powerful wife Kaahumanu and his son Liholiho shared the reign. Liholiho, called Kamehameha II, brought many changes to the kingdom. Kamehameha I had traded sandalwood for considerable wealth, but he kept a tight hold on its harvesting and sale, and used the money to purchase guns and ships to protect his power. When he died his heir spent the revenue in a frantic buying spree. Liholiho allowed other chiefs harvesting rights so they could purchase, not guns, but the fine china and mirrors, the precious jewelry, chandeliers, French wines and brandies, and the dandified clothes they had come to love. They built and furnished great houses. They raped the forests and literally enslaved their people to collect and deliver the sandalwood to waiting ships. Soon many chiefs were in ruinous debt, and their crop began to disappear; the abused workers in the forests destroyed the sandalwood seedlings.

Liholiho could not have ruled without Kaahumanu's help. His most important decisions as king were made with her guidance. Because of her and his mother, Keopuolani, the old system of kapu was abolished. Liholiho ate freely with women, a forbidden practice. He outlawed the ancient ceremonies and ordered every heiau destroyed, every tiki burned. But his pulling down of the old beliefs with no planned structure for new ones began a chain of events that led to the loss of Hawaiian identity and lands.

In 1820, in the spiritual vacuum created by Liholiho's smashing of kapu, the first Christian

SUGAR CANE

A patchwork of cane fields and creeping subdivisions hug some of Kauai's last cinder cones on the Poipu plain. The reservoir is called Waita, an unusual word combining Hawaiian (*wai,* water) and Japanese (*ta,* rice paddy).

missionary company arrived in Hawaii. Their goal was to "save the savages." They would eventually acquire land from the kings and build hundreds of churches. They translated the Bible into Hawaiian, produced the first written form of the language, and took on the task of teaching the people to read. The missionaries were tireless zealots whose strict morality and unwavering belief in the superior God of the Testaments won many converts. Among those baptized in the haole faith were Kaahumanu,

Keopuolani, Kapiolani and other powerful alii. Hawaii soon became a Christina nation, complete with persecution of nonbelievers.

Liholiho loved traveling and decided to journey to the British Isles to see the home of his foreign friends. On November 27, 1823, Kamehameha II, his favorite wife, Kamamalu, and their attendants boarded the English whaling ship *L'Aigle* bound for Britain. In London the Hawaiians attended gala parties in their honor. They beheld the dazzling architecture of this "advanced" culture. But then the royal couple contracted measles. With no immunity whatsoever, both Liholiho and Kamamalu died. The British returned their bodies to Honolulu, to be buried in their homeland.

Liholiho's death brought his younger brother Kauikeaouli to power as Kamehameha III. He was very young, and his long reign was a troubled one. At first he relied on Kaahumanu to rule, but on June 5, 1832, she died. To succeed her in the position of regent (kuhina nui) the missionaries selected Kinau, a half-sister and wife of Liholiho. This was not Kauikeaouli's choice, and he rebelled with drink, gambling and sexual excesses that were frowned on by the elders and the church. The principal reason for the young king's wildness, however, was said to be his love for his sister Nahienaena. The two siblings had been betrothed since birth in a customary arrangement among alii that would ensure "purer" progeny. They lived together as teenagers and were secretly wed, but the Congregational missionaries forced them apart and convinced Nahienaena to marry a "Big Island" chief. She quickly bore a son, most probably sired by her brother. But the baby died within hours, and

HAOLE RELIGION

The European and American missionaries built many churches throughout the islands in their efforts to convert the Hawaiian people to Christianity. This church is located at Milolii in the Kona district of the "Big Island."

the brokenhearted Nahienaena never recovered. She died a few months later, in December 1836. The effect on Kauikeaouli, after many gloomy days of mourning, was to snap him out of his hedonism. When he came of age to officially take the throne, he accepted Kinau as his regent and set about a long reign that was characterized by judiciousness.

As sandalwood stocks dwindled, other trades started. Whaling ships found Hawaii to be a perfect place to make repairs and stock fresh

food and water. Whalers spurred the growth of an increasingly Western economy. Blacksmiths, sailmakers, carpenters, cattle ranchers, farmers, grog shop proprietors, prostitutes and merchants found the ports of Honolulu and Lahaina to be extremely profitable havens. With an increasing foreign population in Hawaii, written laws were needed to help maintain order. Kauikeaouli had a declaration drawn up that defined punishable crimes; the penal code included murder, theft, fraud, sexual misconduct and drunkenness.

Haole commercial enterprise brought with it a notion entirely new to Hawaiians. In the old days all land belonged to the king, who let his subjects use it "on loan." Suddenly every merchant in the nation wanted deeded land. It was just bad business to invest in an establishment without a guarantee of land usage. If the merchants could not buy land they threatened to take their companies away. The new God, as well, required deeds in paradise. Missionary descendants eventually bought such great tracts of land they became the barons of Hawaii's land-based enterprises. As the saying goes, "The missionaries came to do good, and they did well."

American missionaries became important counselors to the king. They advocated stronger ties between the United States and Hawaii, but the British and French would not release their claim to the islands. Lord George Paulet, through a series of power moves, wore down Kauikeaouli and replaced the Hawaiian flag with the British Union Jack. This lasted about five months. London again rescinded the cession

MOANA HOTEL

The recently restored Moana Hotel. Built in 1901 of Douglas fir from the Pacific Northwest, the Moana was Waikiki's first "country hotel," so far from downtown Honolulu it had its own icehouse and electric plant. On this day a shadow cast by the west tower of the Hyatt Regency cuts across the Moana's north wing and its famous banyan tree, planted in 1886.

conducted by one of its captains. Both France and Britain, long known for their mutual mistrust, shortly after declared Hawaii an independent state. Mounting interest on sandalwood debts pushed the young government into a financial hurricane. Income was collected without record, and accounting in general was poor. But as Hawaiians and foreigners added branches to the evolving constitutional

monarchy, the government became more effective.

In 1846 a Land Commission began to set up a means to validate land claims and opened a test market for fee simple tracts on Maui and Oahu. They offered the parcels to the commoners and explained the concept of free and clear ownership. The commoners bought all of the available land in those tracts. With this response, Kamehameha III and his counselors were faced with the problem of dividing the remaining lands fairly among the people of Hawaii.

In March 1848 the Great Mahele, or Land Division, was held. The king received parcels for his private use, and the remaining land was divided three ways: government lands, chief lands and commoner lands. The legislature of 1850 gave the right of land ownership to foreigners as well,

an act that prompted a revival of industry. Markets flourished. Whaling, sugar, cattle and coffee boomed. The government's gross income soared.

Good times encouraged religion and education. Protestant missionaries built Punahou School in Honolulu for their children. The Mission Seminary at Lahainaluna on Maui expanded. Mokuaikaua Church in Kailua-Kona went up, as did the mission schoolhouse in Honolulu, the Catholic Normal School in Ahuimanu, Oahu, the first Mormon chapel in Pulehu, Maui, and a number of common schools for the children of the kingdom. By 1866 English was the language of instruction in all schools in Hawaii.

In 1853 a smallpox epidemic hit the islands and claimed at least 6,000 lives, most of them Hawaiian. The disease was the latest in a series of introduced

HAWAIIAN RANCH
A corner of eucalyptus marks a high pasture at Waikii Ranch on the "Big Island."

illnesses that devastated the Hawaiian people. Because of their isolated development, the islanders had no immunities against foreign germs. Captain Cook's sailors had introduced venereal disease, which spread so quickly through the free-loving, bisexual society that when Cook returned to Hawaii in 1779 he discovered to his horror that the syphilis and gonorrhea his men had left on Kauai a year before had spread to Maui and the Big Island. Over the next hundred years foreigners brought to Hawaii deadly strains of measles, influenza, tuberculosis and other

diseases, the last and most terrifying of which was the mai-Pake ("Chinese disease" or leprosy). Not until the late nineteenth century would disease rates slow among the native population. By then most people with Hawaiian blood had other bloods as well, and today the number of "pure" Hawaiians is counted only in the hundreds.

On December 15, 1854, Kauikeaouli died, and Alexander Liholiho was crowned king. He was 20 years old. Five years earlier he had traveled to Europe and America with his brother Lot Kamehameha.

Hawaii was undergoing a new period of upheaval. France had begun negotiations for another land treaty; sugar interests imported foreign workers from China; the United States was moving toward civil war; and the native Hawaiian population had decreased to only 70,000 by 1855, down from perhaps 600,000 or so when Cook arrived. Kamehameha IV set about the multiple tasks of encouraging commerce and agriculture, strengthening the schools for Hawaiian children, improving roads and harbors, and establishing in 1859, with his wife's help, the edifice that would be a lasting monument to their rule: the Queen's Hospital.

On May 20, 1858, King Kamehameha IV and Queen Emma had a son. They named him Prince Albert Edward Kauikeaouli Leiopapa a Kamehameha, and hoped his birth was a blessing from God and a sign that the Hawaiian race would be increased. The whole country celebrated the birth of the heir. But only four years later Prince Albert contracted a sudden fever and died. He was the last child in the line of succession of the Great Kamehameha. Following the death of his son, the king fell into a depression that, coupled with asthma, finally killed him at the age of twenty-nine.

In 1863 Alexander's older brother Lot, the last ruler of the royal line of Kamehameha I, ascended the throne as Kamehameha V. Lot was strong willed and powerful, and he took it upon himself to reclaim the authority of the crown that had been given away by Kauikeaouli. He refused to recognize the Constitution of 1852, stating that he would write another, and he appointed a cabinet that shared his views. With the new constitution, Lot Kamehameha addressed national dignity, strength in the foreign arena, and literacy and land requirements for voting.

Commerce expanded under Kamehameha V. A new post office and government offices were built,

COLONIAL FORT

Fort Elizabeth, named for the wife of Russian emperor Alexander I, combines a star-shaped Russian-designed fort and traditional Kauai stonework. This was the fourth fort begun in the islands by Dr Georg Anton Scheffer, the agent for the imperial Russian government. The first was started at Honolulu Harbor in 1816 and completed by Kamehameha after he expelled the Russians from Oahu. A year later two smaller forts at Hanalei on Kauai's north shore, and this stronghold on Waimea River, built with the cooperation of High Chief Kaumualii, raised Kamehameha's ire again and he deported the Russians from the kingdom. For more than a year (1816–17) the Russian flag had flown over Kauai.

along with Iolani Barracks, a quarantine station and an insane asylum. By the 1860s petroleum had cut into the whale oil market with a cheaper, cleaner substitute, and sugar took over as Hawaii's major industry. The growth of the plantations and the dwindling of the native Hawaiian population forced the sugar barons to bring in more Asians to work the fields.

Although he was urged to do so for the sake of producing an heir, Kamehameha V never married. The Constitution of 1864 named his sister Victoria Kamamalu successor, but she died in 1866. On his forty-third birthday Lot fell victim to an unexpected, fast-moving illness. From his deathbed came no statement of who should be his successor, and the mighty line of Kamehamehas ended.

In 1873 Hawaii held its first election to name a king. The winner was William C. Lunalilo,

a personable member of the alii class whose great wit made him a popular monarch. But he too fell ill, in November of that year when he was in Kailua-Kona on the "Big Island," and upon his return to Honolulu in February 1874 he died. His reign had lasted only 13 months. He was interred in the Lunalilo Mausoleum adjoining the Kawaiahao Church. In his honor, and by the terms of his will, the government established Lunalilo Home for the poor and ailing people of Hawaiian ancestry.

Following the death of Lunalilo, another election pitted two strong candidates against each other: Queen Emma (the widow of Kamehameha IV) and David Kalakaua. On February 12, 1874, the Legislative Assembly elected Kalakaua to the throne, possibly because his opponent advocated stronger ties to Britain. Queen

INFAMOUS KEALAKEKUA
Kealakekua Bay, Hawaii, where Captain Cook made his final port of call. In a skirmish on shore the Hawaiians killed Cook. It was 8:00 AM, February 14, 1779.

Emma's supporters were enraged and stormed the courthouse. British and American marines landed, called in from three vessels in Honolulu Harbor. They put down the riot and remained ashore for a week while the new regime became established.

Kalakaua was a peaceful man. His wife, Queen Kapiolani, accompanied him on his trips throughout the island chain to speak to his people. He urged them to work hard for the betterment of the kingdom, but his strongest message was for the

Hawaiians to restore their culture and increase their numbers. For the first time in many years, since the missionaries had compelled laws against it, the hula was performed for the king.

Kalakaua petitioned the United States for support, requesting a reciprocity treaty stating that no other country would have dominion over the islands. The treaty opened free trade for sugar with the United States and eventually gave the American navy the right to use the Pearl River Harbor. But although he acknowledged and hoped to benefit from American power, Kalakaua preferred to pattern his government after European monarchies. He built the very Victorian and resplendent Iolani Palace and held there a grand coronation following his trip around the world. The jeweled crowns that the king set upon his own head and Kapiolani's were worn only at the coronation and never again. Mark Twain characterized the ceremony as "all the workings of an ocean liner crammed into a sardine can."

For all the good Kalakaua did to preserve Hawaiian culture by recording ancient legends and restoring the hula to social prominence, his regime became riddled with corruption and scandal. Walter Murray Gibson, a brilliant but misguidedly self-serving politico, came to Hawaii originally as an emissary of the Mormon Church, and soon ingratiated himself with the government. He became Kalakaua's principal adviser, and in 10 years the two of them drove the national debt up from $388,900 to $2,600,000. Nearly all the foreigners and many native Hawaiians became disenchanted with the government.

A group of disgruntled businessmen formed a secret organization: the Hawaiian League. In 1887 they armed themselves and in a show of force made Kalakaua sign a new constitution called the Bayonet Constitution, which extended greater powers to the legislature and provided voting rights for resident haoles. Gibson was arrested and allowed to leave the country; he died in San Francisco six months later. After three more years in which factions for native rule vied against foreign businessmen, Kalakaua fell ill and also traveled to San Francisco, hoping a change of climate would restore his health. It did not. He died there on January 20, 1891, and his sister Liliuokalani was proclaimed queen. She was the last native Hawaiian monarch to reign over the islands.

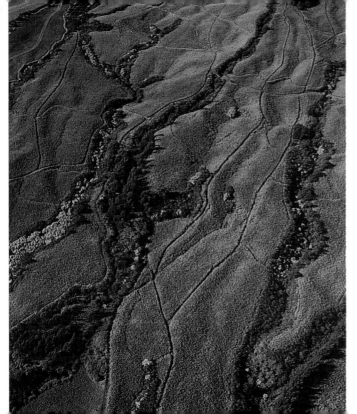

CANEFIELD PATTERNS

Sugar cane was introduced to Hawaii by the Polynesians centuries ago. It was only after the arrival of Westerners that the plant was cultivated. The islands have an ideal climate for growing this crop. Canefields, such as this one at Hamakua on Hawaii, flourish.

ARCHITECTURE

Some of the earliest examples of Western architecture in the Hawaiian Islands are the churches the missionaries began building almost as soon as they arrived in the 1820s. They built churches of all shapes and sizes, some made from wood and others from stone. As Western influence increased throughout the islands, traditional methods of building were abandoned. Western-style homes and farms sprung up, and later plantations and factories. Early, ramshackle towns grew into small cities. King Kalakaua, who wished to style his monarchy after the European models, built the Iolani Palace in order to imitate the grandiose palaces of Europe.

Architecture

RESTORED CHURCH
The recently restored Huialoha
("gathering of love") Church, at Kaupo
in east Maui, was built in 1859 as a
Congregational "circuit" church.

196

"THE CARPENTER PRIEST"

Father Damien, known as "the carpenter priest" because of all the churches he built in Hawaii, established this one, St. Joseph's, in Kamalo, Molokai, in 1876 (left). To the right of the chapel entrance, a lei-draped statue of Damien casts a familiar shadow.

MORMON TEMPLE

Burdened with the epithets "Taj Mahal of the Pacific" and "Hawaii's Lincoln Memorial," the Mormon Temple at Laie, Oahu (right) faces east down a Norfolk pine–bordered avenue that runs straight to the ocean. Laie became a gathering place for Latter-day Saints in 1864, after the church lost its ownership of Lanai. Labor missionaries erected the temple in 1919.

THE DOLE PINEAPPLE
Probably the most famous water tower in the world, the Dole pineapple (left) was erected above the Honolulu pineapple cannery in 1928. Turn the photo upside down and see the faces on the pineapple sections.

ALONG THE KONA COAST
Private houses not far from the "City of Refuge" on the Kona Coast (right). Modern versions of the traditional Hawaiian outrigger canoes, with outboard motors, are popular.

AN UNUSUAL DESIGN
The Holy Ghost Hall in Kula on Maui
(left) is an unusual octagonal shape.
This church was established in 1897.

A MODERN FARM
A Western style farm on the Keenai
Peninsula on Maui (above).

A CHURCH AT KEENAI
This church on the Keenai Peninsula, Maui (left), is further evidence of the enthusiasm of the Christian missionaries for building.

BUDDHIST TEMPLE
A Buddhist temple in Honolulu, Oahu (right). This port city has historically been a mixing pot of many cultures and religions.

NATURAL POWER
Tides and waves challenge this ramshackle kauhale (cluster of dwellings) on the south Kona coast of the "Big Island." Notice the dog, the TV antenna, and the white roof weighted down by lava rock.

HISTORIC CHURCHES

Most Western missionaries believed in the superiority of their religion and culture. They were determined to replace the traditional Hawaiian beliefs and practices with their particular version of Christianity. They began building churches almost as soon as they arrived in the islands. The unusual cross-shaped church (left) is in Honolulu, Oahu. The wooden church (right) at Koloa, Kauai was built in 1835.

AGRICULTURE
AND
INDUSTRY

The arrival of Western agriculture had significant environmental impacts on the islands. Westerners brought with them non-native animals and plants which threatened local flora and fauna, much of which is found nowhere else in the world. The new agricultural practices employed by the Westerners were not as sustainable as the traditional Hawaiian system. Kamehameha the Great began trading sandalwood in the early nineteenth century. However, this plant was soon exhausted and whaling, which the haoles introduced, became the predominant industry. After the decline of whaling, the cultivation of sugar cane and pineapples developed as staple industries.

"EXOTIC" ANIMALS

Europeans brought many plants and animals with them when they settled in Hawaii, as had the Polynesians before them. These cattle are waiting to be sold at the cattle yards near Waimea on the "Big Island" (left).

CLEARING CANEFIELDS

In this canefield near Hanapepe, Kauai (right), egrets have learned to follow tractors for the bugs they expose. Burned sugar cane stalks are loaded into trucks and hauled to the mill.

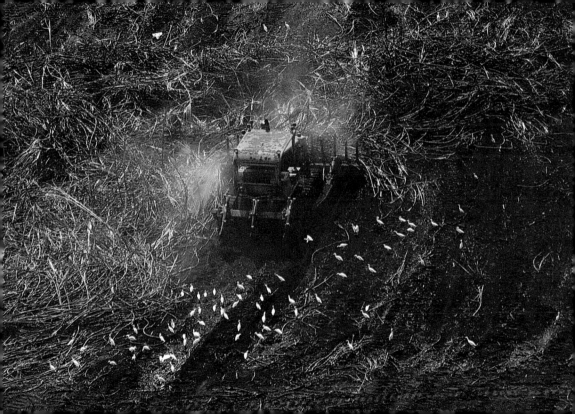

PINEAPPLE PLANTATIONS

One of the many plants introduced by Westerners is the pineapple. This plant was in evidence in Hawaii from the early 1800s. The fruit is now successfully grown in commerical plantations such as this one on Oahu (left). Pineapples are mechanically harvested in the Wahiawa area of Oahu (right). It was in this area that Jim Dole established the first plantation of the famous Hawaiian Pineapple Company in the early 1900s.

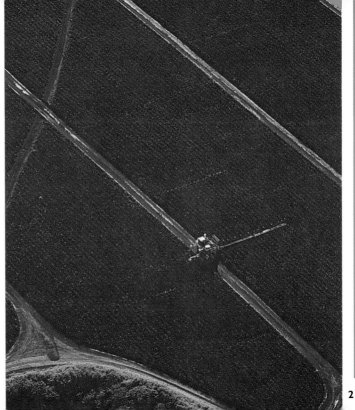

REFINING SUGAR

The Waialua Sugar Mill (left), one of two remaining cane mills on Oahu (the other is in Waipahu), was built in 1897. The striped bin near the smokestack stores bagasse (the dried pulp of juiced sugar cane stalks), which is used to fuel the mill's furnaces.

WORKING THE LAND

Workers preparing a field in Wahiawa, Oahu (right) for a new crop of pineapple. When Europeans, Americans and Asians came to Hawaii they brought plows and other machines that worked the land harder than the hands and digging sticks of the native Hawaiians. By the twentieth century, sugar and pineapple covered most of the arable land that makes up seven percent of Hawaii's total acreage.

FARMING ON OAHU
A truck farm in Waianae Valley, Oahu (above). Although enough arable land exists on the islands to meet Hawaii's market needs, 75 percent of the produce consumed in the state is imported.

FIELDS OF FIRE
The sugar cane fields are burnt before the harvest begins on Kilohan plantation in Lihue, Kauai (right).

MACADAMIA ORCHARDS
The Mauna Loa macadamia orchards south of Hilo on the "Big Island" (above), unlike other "mac" farms, feature tightly planted trees surrounded by Norfolk pine windbreaks. The lime-colored plots in the nursery are the young macadamia seedlings.

GROWING FLOWERS
A flower farm on Oahu (right). With its tradition of lei giving, Hawaii is one of the world's most "flowerful" lands. The flora here are as varied and beautiful as the island's landscapes.

NON-NATIVE MACADAMIAS
The macadamia nuts for which Hawaii has become renowned are not indigenous. The plant was introduced to the islands from Australia by William Purvis in 1882. At plantations such as this on Hawaii (left) macadamias are successfully grown.

PRODUCING PINEAPPLES
Rows of pineapples on a plantation in the Leilehua district of Oahu (right).

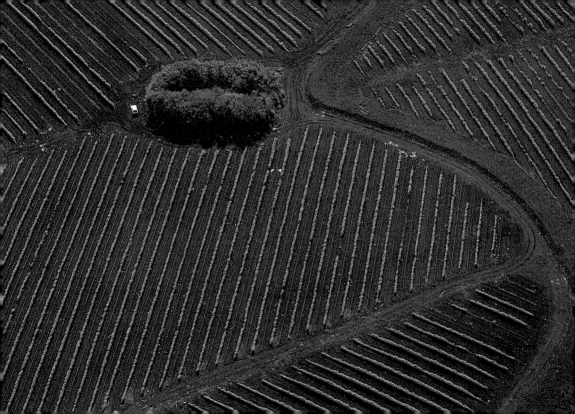

YOUNG CANE
These bright green rows of sugar cane on Kauai (left) have been newly planted.

KALAIMANA POINT
A patchwork of fields at Kalaimana Point on Kauai (above).

KUKUI AND CANE

Like a broken haku lei, a kukui-laden streambed crosses a cane field at Hamakua, Hawaii.

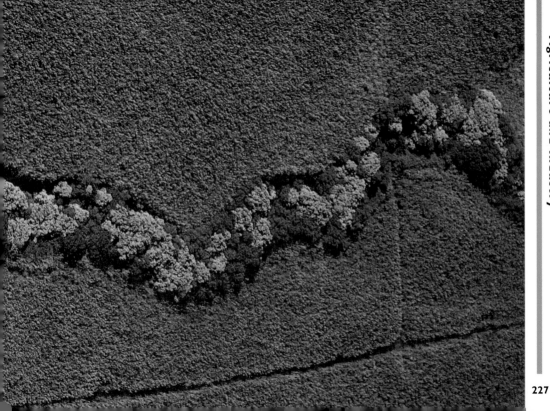

IDYLLIC PASTURES
The title of this masterpiece: *Blue Tidal Pool, Red-layered Sea Cliff and Yellow Field with Cattle*. Near Paia, Maui (left).

A CANE FIRE
A cane fire near the Wailua River on Kauai (right). Sugar cane workers wait until the winds are right to help them direct the flames. The sugar is easier to harvest after it has been burned.

MEN AT WORK
Pouring cement for a new irrigation system in a canefield east of Waimea, Kauai (left), these workers take a break to smile for the photographer in the helicopter.

AN ORDERED ORCHARD
The straight lines of orchard rows on a farm near Lihu, the capital of Kauai (right).

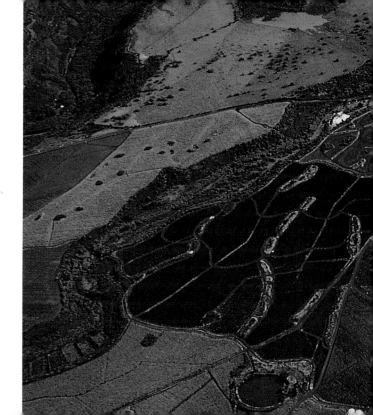

Agriculture and Industry

FERTILE FIELDS

The rich pastures of the Kalaheo district on Kauai are well supplied with water from the many streams which run through the area. Parts of this area were first leased from Kamehameha III in the 1860s by a Scotsman named Duncan McBryde to start a cattle ranch. At one stage the Kauai Pineapple Company had plantations in the district. The major crops now grown in the area are sugar cane and coffee.

PART FOUR

MODERN HAWAII

ABOUT
MODERN HAWAII

In the late nineteenth century the last of the Hawaiian monarchs, Queen Liliuokalani, was overthrown and the islands were annexed by the United States. The twentieth century saw major social and political changes—the plantations flourished and many new workers arrived from Asia and Europe, which significantly altered the social make-up of the islands. Hawaii became a focal point for the U.S. military during the Second World War. In the post-war years the idea of statehood was championed and in 1959 the islands became the fiftieth state in the Union.

ABOUT MODERN HAWAII

Queen Liliuokalani, known for her musical talent, her regal dignity and the tragedy of her reign, struggled to preserve her people's sovereignty and watched helplessly as the islands were stolen by American forces.

AN ALOHA FROM KONA
Not far from some of the most remarkable petroglyph fields in Hawaii, these greetings in Kailua-Kona offer their own kind of expression. Aloha means "hello," "goodbye" and "love."

Actually, the bloodless, day-long revolution that overthrew the queen was not engineered by the U.S. government. In 1887, before Queen Liliuokalani ascended the throne, Hawaii's haole community had imposed its Bayonet Constitution to curtail the monarchy. Liliuokalani wanted to be more than a figurehead ruler of her people and announced her intention to abolish the Bayonet Constitution and reclaim her powers. This alarmed the planters and merchants, who feared for their prosperity and the long-hoped-for annexation of Hawaii to the United States. They organized a hasty and secret committee—the Committee of Safety—that decided that only the end of the monarchy could protect haole interests.

Aided by the U.S. minister to the kingdom of Hawaii, John L. Stevens, the committee organized a provisional government. One hundred sixty marines from a visiting American gunship stood ready to man artillery positions. The mere show of firepower was enough. On January 16, 1893, Liliuokalani submitted to the committee's order to abdicate the throne. Iolani Palace became the seat of the new government, headed by Judge Sanford B. Dole.

When U.S. President Grover Cleveland learned of the overthrow, he denounced it. But it was too late. Neither Cleveland nor his new emissary, James Blount, could dismantle the provisional government and restore the queen's power. Cleveland did, however, refuse to consider annexing Hawaii to the United States. The haole politicians created a new constitution and a new, sovereign Republic of Hawaii. And they waited until July 7, 1898, when

the new administration of William McKinley signed a Joint Resolution of Annexation and made Hawaii a U.S. territory.

To the planters, annexation meant development, and growth sweetened the sugar and new pineapple industries. Plantations grew. Additional workers arrived from Japan, China, the Philippines and Europe. Most immigrants came from Japan, and, though as laborers they received few rights, the Japanese and their descendants would grow to dominate government and education in Hawaii.

Along with the housing provided by the plantations, slum areas like Chinatown emerged around Honolulu to accommodate the large numbers of poor immigrants. Overcrowding and lack of sanitation made Chinatown a hotbed of troubles. In 1899 an epidemic of imported

bubonic plague broke out; Board of Health officials began to burn certain rat-infested buildings in the area. On January 20, 1900, one of the fires got out of control and blazed for three days over 38 acres (15 ha) of Chinatown, leaving thousands of people homeless. The famous Chinatown fire did not manage to halt the plague, however, which continued in Honolulu for three more months.

The day the plague's end was announced, April 30, also marked the beginning of a new political era. President McKinley's administration passed the Organic Act, a document that established the form of Hawaii's government for the next 59 years. The terms of the act would be modified later to give island citizens a more just balance of rights and responsibilities, but the stable framework would endure,

DIAMOND HEAD
Diamond Head got its modern name in 1825 when British sailors hiking the slopes found some worthless calcite crystals and thought they were diamonds. Points of interest here (clockwise): Hawaii National Guard buildings (inside the crater), Diamond Head Road, Diamond Head Lighthouse, the Gold Coast, Kapiolani Park, Waikiki, the Ala Wai Golf Course and lower Kaimuki, a suburb.

gradually replacing the monarchy in citizens' minds.

Early voting laws provided means to exclude Asians from political participation. However the plantations continued to bring in Asian laborers. In 1901, James D. Dole established the Hawaiian Pineapple Company, opening successful markets on the U.S. mainland. Soon after, in 1904, a group of Hawaiian sugar growers

gained control of a California sugar refinery, establishing the California and Hawaiian Sugar Refining Corporation.

The increasing consolidation of agricultural interest coupled with poor wages and working conditions led to increasing labor dissatisfaction and, inevitably, to workers' unions. At first, laborers grouped themselves by nationality. The Japanese proved most actively militant, organizing at least 14 strikes between 1902 and 1905. Slowly they succeeded in improving labor conditions and wages, and their effectiveness foreshadowed the future victories of the ILWU (International Longshoremen's and Warehousemen's Union), the AFL and the CIO. Also foreshadowed, perhaps, was the effectiveness of the Japanese at political activity.

Though many years would pass before it reached its lofty position

as Hawaii's premier industry, tourism began in Hawaii by the early twentieth century. The Moana Hotel, on Waikiki Beach, opened its doors to visitors in 1901 and was followed 26 years later by the grand, pink Royal Hawaiian Hotel. The hinterland of Waikiki then was a tranquil marsh, not to be fully drained until the late 1920s, when the Ala Wai Canal was dug.

Conservation in the islands also traces its roots to the early years of the century. In 1909, President Theodore Roosevelt declared the Northwestern Hawaiian Islands a national wildlife refuge. Hawaiian prince Jonah Kuhio Kalanianaole, the territorial delegate to Congress, was concerned as well with the conservation of the Hawaiian race. He sponsored the Hawaiian Homes Commission Act, which marked 200,000 acres (80,000 ha) to be allocated to needy Hawaiians

who had been dispossessed by takeovers of their land. Hawaiians of at least 50 percent native blood were encouraged to apply for inexpensive leases on agricultural and pastoral lands. But because of bureaucracy and mismanagement the program failed. Less than five percent of the allocated land was actually leased to Hawaiians. Only recently have there been signs that the commitments would finally be honored, but to date an estimated 30,000 people have died while on the Hawaiian Homes waiting list.

Another foundation laid during this period promoted the ascendance of the "Big Five"— large corporations that began as factors or agent companies of the sugar interests but expanded to gain holdings in public utilities, shipping, banks, department stores, resort development companies and other concerns. The "Big Five" are Amfac

A SURFER'S PARADISE

A surfer rides the relatively gentle waves off Waikiki Beach, Oahu. Hawaii is renowned for its surf, particularly the spectacular powerful "pipeline" on the north shore of Oahu. The islands are host to many surfing tournaments and have become a mecca for surfers from all around the world.

(American Factor; it has now been sold to mainland interests), C. Brewer, Alexander and Baldwin, Castle and Cooke, and Theo. H. Davies. Though smaller businesses were able to coexist with these giants, the "Big Five" set the rules for Hawaiian commerce and exercised considerable control over the island economy and politics.

In the antitrust atmosphere of the Depression era, the "Big Five" and affiliated interests faced economic competition. Matson Navigation, a "Big Five"-backed company, enjoyed dominance of the freight and passenger shipping business in Hawaii through 1938, but even its monopoly was finally challenged. Hawaii's big business and political communities are still charged with cronyism today. Outsiders can usually find a niche in the corridors of power, however, and by today's estimates 95 percent of the registered businesses in Hawaii employ five or fewer people.

World War II propelled Hawaii onto the international scene. Japan's bombs on December 7, 1941, not only damaged the U.S. Pacific fleet at Pearl Harbor, they also exploded the lives of Hawaii's people. Many Japanese Americans in the islands, like those on the mainland West Coast, were interned in camps. The Pacific war brought an influx of American soldiers for duty assignments and R&R. And throughout the war, Hawaii's citizens were subject to martial law—including military courts and the suspension of habeas corpus.

Despite hardship, and despite persistent doubts about the annexation only 43 years before, Hawaii responded to the war with patriotism and dedication. Thousands of Americans of Japanese ancestry (AJAs)

OBSERVATORY AT HALEAKELA
A road winds across the barren landscape near Haleakela Crater on Maui, to the observatories of Science City.

volunteered for active military service. Soldiers in the 100th Battalion and the 442nd Regimental Combat Team, in particular, were highly decorated and praised for uncommon bravery in the European theater. Other AJAs enlisted as interpreters and undoubtedly saved thousands of lives by intercepting enemy messages. Back home, citizens bought war bonds, submitted to rationing, and offered cheer and hospitality to soldiers. And the sugar and pineapple industries

gave not only their crops but also laborers and machinery to the war effort.

Hawaii's contribution to the Second World War was crucial, and its people demonstrated an extraordinary allegiance to the United States. Following the end of the war, the cause of statehood was all the more easily defended, and in 1959 President Eisenhower signed the long-awaited legislation naming Hawaii the fiftieth state of the union. The same year, jet service from California to Hawaii was inaugurated, cutting travel time from nine hours to less than five. The doors to the tourism boom were thrown wide.

Hawaii's postwar, early statehood period also saw the decline of the Republican party, champions of big business and vested interests, and the emergence of the Democrats as the party of power. The change can be attributed to the political energy of the Japanese–American community. Local Japanese are conscientious voters who tend to vote en bloc. After years of subordination as plantation laborers, they developed an allegiance to the labor-friendly Democratic party.

In 1963, John A. Burns became the first in a line of Democratic governors to dominate Hawaiian politics. Burns had spoken in defense of the loyalty and rights of Hawaii's Japanese during World War II; as a result, he enjoyed their critical support in gaining the governorship. Burns's successor, George Ariyoshi, became the first American of Japanese ancestry to be governor of an American state. Ariyoshi served three terms starting in 1974 and passed the office to the next Democrat, John Waihee, who was the first person of native Hawaiian ancestry to be elected governor of the islands.

After two hundred years of pursuing things new, Hawaii in recent years has begun to reassess the value of things old. Sparked by John Dominis Holt's book *On Being Hawaiian* and by resurging interest in ancient crafts, chants and hulas, native Hawaiians and non-Hawaiians alike have discovered a new passion for the values of traditional island culture. The Hawaiian Renaissance is celebrated through hula and native art

THE FINISH LINE
The finish line of a walking race at McCoy Park on Oahu. The islands play host to many international sporting events each year. Perhaps the best-known is the gruelling "Hawaiian Iron Man" endurance race.

festivals and Hawaiian language study; a growing activist movement focuses on preserving cultural sites and natural resources, and on the restoration of Hawaiian sovereignty.

A hundred years ago the sun shone on an island kingdom where Hawaiian monarchs ruled their own people. The land was unmarred by highways and high rises. In the hands of American planters, pineapple and sugar flourished. Today the sun shines on a modern American state, governed according to American tradition. Shores and valleys bear the thorny crowns of sky-scraping hotels, condominium complexes and office buildings. Roadways cut through ancient mountains and watersheds. The current major crop is tourists; the millions who travel to this wonderland outnumber Hawaii's residents nearly six to one.

In the far-flung areas, na kuaaina (upcountry retreats) retain a timeless grace and enchanting beauty. But as more people crowd the islands even the most remote forests are threatened. The 1990s witnessed a struggle between those who would save our precious lands and those who would pave them. Hawaii's roads swarm with cars. On Kauai, the "Garden Isle," the biggest problem is traffic. On Oahu, if all the cars on the island hit the street at the same time, every inch of asphalt from Waikiki to the North Shore would be covered.

In many ways we have reached a saturation point. Today's population in Hawaii, including residents and a tourist count that constantly renews itself, has reached the level at which our natural resources—especially water—are being used beyond capacity. Attendant upon the

population increase is a host of varied environmental problems. Every ecological danger on Earth is played out locally in Hawaii.

To describe what man's accelerating industries are costing the planet there has come a neologism: terracide. It means killing the Earth. In Hawaii our terracidal activities range from overdevelopment to release of man-made toxins into the air and water. Oahu's petroleum-burning power plants and our chemical factories, jet planes and automobiles pollute the atmosphere. Tanker ships occasionally spill oil into the ocean. The islands' natural reservoirs of fresh water are increasingly threatened, as exemplified by Oahu's aquifer.

The two mountain ranges on Oahu pull in rainwater from cloud-bearing trade winds and deposit some of it in a pool

MARINA AT HONOLULU

Fishing trawlers and commercial cruisers moored with recreational boats at a marina in Honolulu, on Oahu.

floating within a lens on the saltwater-permeated bedrock of the island. The lens, contained by reef and ocean and capped by lava, was formerly the purest body of water ever discovered. "Formerly" because toxins from pineapple and sugar plantations, road maintenance, marijuana spraying, golf courses, and industry have polluted it.

Now the water system is further threatened by new highway construction and tunneling. The two tunnels already piercing the Koolau Range have affected the basalt infrastructure of the old volcano, accelerated draining and caused the upper elevations of the mountains to dry measurably. Water is gregarious. When the peaks contain water they attract more, pulling the moisture from the clouds. Further tunneling causes additional drying on the peaks, limiting rain catchment and reducing the island's water supply.

"Hahai no ka ua i ka ululau," the Hawaiians say, "the rain always follows the forest." It is not just the mountains but the trees that bring in the rains. Knowing this, the early Hawaiians went into the high forest and cut down only the trees they needed. They developed a more responsible husbandry because for them the land was—and still is—a sacred manifestation of the gods. A place to be cooperated with rather than subjugated, a place to be bound to. As a modern people we have the technological power to completely sever what binds us to the planet. We can replace a forest of rain-gathering, oxygen-producing, medicine-rich flora with a river of internal combustion engines. We can replace the clear air and clouds with smog, the water with oil, the birds with nothing.

THE ISLANDS' CAPITOL
The landmarks of two governments: the Hawaii State Capitol and Iolani Palace. The architects of the capitol designed the building with columns that suggest royal palms, conic legislative chambers like volcanoes, and a moat to make it an island, but some Hawaiians say it looks like a squid or jellyfish sneaking up behind the Victorian-style palace.

What is already lost to urbanization has brought particular suffering to native Hawaiians. Dana Naone Hall, an Hawaiian activist and poet who has fought for native Hawaiian rights on Maui, articulates the position of her people: "The immense changes wrought by large-scale economic interests, while in many ways beneficial have also been primarily

responsible for the destruction of the Hawaiian environment and native Hawaiian culture. For Hawaiians, reverence for our ancestors is the same as reverence for the land. This points us in the right direction if we want to protect what is beautiful and mysterious about the place where we live."

At the end of the twentieth century, the people of Hawaii understand that we are beginning a new age. Today we know more about the islands than ever before, how they grew out of the ocean and gave birth to this most diverse and astonishingly beautiful environment. We know how the human presence here has altered the life and spirit of Hawaii, and we understand the value of what we must preserve here.

Our choices have never been clearer. Sometimes we make the right ones. As a collective society

Hawaii is a model. There is remarkable ethnic harmony in these islands where no group constitutes a majority. Grown from native and plantation cultures, Hawaii has become a modern place, with greater educational and employment opportunities for its people. It is the only state with a universal health system. It has more support programs for senior citizens than any other state. It is the only state with a subsidized after-school program for children. It has developed new industries, including aquaculture and selected high-technology enterprises. It is the home of a burgeoning film industry, fine museums, and study centers, with advanced research in oceanography, astronomy and Pacific-Asian affairs. Environmental issues are important too. Hawaii is the only state without billboards cluttering the roads, and the local

SHIPWRECK BEACH
The 1960 wreck of a Navy concrete-hulled YO (yard oiler) tank barge lies on the reef of Shipwreck Beach on the north shore of Lanai.

governments in the last 10 years have acquired thousands of acres of land for conservation, park and recreational use. The privately funded Nature Conservancy has reserved huge tracts of pristine rain forest.

Local political leaders are sensitive to maintaining a guard against those developers who would tear the place asunder. "Preserving the pure naturalness of Hawaii's mountains, valleys, air, beaches and water is vital to life here for us all," said Frank Fasi,

when he was mayor of Honolulu. "We depend upon Hawaii's unspoiled riches, not only for our major industry, tourism, but also for our very soul. The beauty of Hawaii drew many of our ancestors here. It keeps us here too. Those of us in positions of public trust must be constantly aware of the threat 'progress' poses to our Aloha state and people."

U.S. Congressman Neil Abercrombie, who frequently opposed Fasi on major issues, agreed with him on this position: "All culture begins with world consciousness, and no people on Earth were and are more acutely aware of this than the Polynesians who found Hawaii and whose lives measure its vitality today. For the Hawaiians, the dictum of Kamehameha III—The Life of the Land is Perpetuated in Righteousness—is more than an admonition, it is the core value of communal existence. While land is inanimate in Western cosmology, an object to be controlled, manipulated and dominated, it is for the Hawaiians a living reality with which humankind must be in harmony. The task in our contemporary world is to make this manifest in ways that do not mock this imperative. The alternative," Abercrombie warned, "is nothing short of revenge by the land as we career into modernity."

The right choice is a simple one. We must commit ourselves to keeping a wise husbandry in Hawaii, to consult with this beauty that is like no other, and to learn what the Hawaiians of old knew so well: to give back what we take. As Governor John Waihe'e has so eloquently observed: "We need to ask ourselves how our ancestors did so much with so little, and why we are able to do so little with so much. When it comes to

"WHITE CITY"

From the time it started to grow in the early nineteenth century, Honolulu was known as a "white city" because its buildings were made of coral block. This view is from above Tantalus and Makiki Heights.

the environment, let us remember our inseparability with nature. We are these islands, the sky and the sea, and it is our responsibility to take action which breathes life into the natural world around us. Let others discover what we already know: that our Earth is a precious and glorious island of the universe, and humankind is her guardian."

E ola no, e-e. Life, give us life.

254

ARCHITECTURE

Hawaii has long been a favorite of the wealthy, who built luxurious mansions around the islands. These estates stand in contrast to the modest dwellings in which most of the local people live. The post-war growth of the tourist industry in Hawaii made a significant impact on the architectural shape of the islands. The need to accommodate the thousands of tourists who visit each year led to development of many high-rise hotels and apartments, particularly at Waikiki Beach. Older-style hotels, like the famous Royal Hawaiian, are now overshadowed by these skyscrapers. As the population increases, the urban areas continue to expand and further encroach on the fragile environment.

WORLD-FAMOUS WAIKIKI
Developers of Waikiki, needing dry
ground to build on, began a public
relations campaign against the marshes,
streams, pools, taro ponds and rice
fields that lay inland from the beach.
In 1919 they began diverting Waikiki's
waters into an artificial canal called
Ala Wai (water path). Lack of
circulation has caused the water to
stagnate, and it is unsafe for swimming.

THE CONTESSA
Variously described as a cement beehive or a stack of coasters, the Contessa condominium (left) rises high above Moiliili, a suburb near the University of Hawaii.

A LUXURIOUS HOME
A home in Kahala (right), a Honolulu suburb. Although oceanside pools are today a fairly common feature of such ritzy estates, they were once pooh-poohed by the have-nots as needlessly extravagant.

HOUSING DEVELOPMENTS
A basic, three-model, low-income tract
has gone up on a Kauai flatland (left).
The red dirt of the region has tinted
the roads and driveways.

THE GOOD LIFE
Life couldn't be simpler for the nautical
resident of this Keehi Lagoon shack
(right) made of old shipping crates
and corrugated tin. However, the
serenity of the place is periodically
broken. It sits beneath the jetway of
Honolulu International Airport.

LAIE POINT

Windward Oahu's Laie Point (left) is a favorite spot for local anglers. Legend says this used to be a giant moo (dragon-lizard) that the demigods Kana and Niheu killed and chopped up. The rock islands to the left are two of the five nearby islands that are the moo chunks thrown into the sea.

OVERDEVELOPMENT ON OAHU

Like a collective statement of postmodern opulence, a community of mansions is rapidly covering Hawaiiloa Ridge (right), above Aina Haina on south Oahu.

BEACH SHACKS
Corrugated iron shacks on a beach
(left) along the Kona Coast on the
"Big Island."

"MILLIONAIRES' ROW"
Expensive and luxurious beach-front
homes (right), with swimming pools
and tennis courts, at Kailua on Oahu.
This strip of beach is known as
"millionaires' row."

THE DUKE ESTATE
Part of the resplendent estate of the tobacco heiress Doris Duke, "the world's richest girl," at Black Point (left), just east of Diamond Head. Hers was the first swimming pool built so close to Oahu's shoreline.

TOURIST ATTRACTIONS
A shuttle boat and tram tracks highlight the immaculate grounds and waterways of the Hyatt Regency Waikoloa on the "Big Island" (right).

THE WAIKIKI YACHT CLUB
Located in a prime position near
Waikiki Beach, the Waikiki Yacht Club
(left) is overshadowed by high-rise
hotels and apartment buildings.

SEA LIFE PARK
Waiting for the morning's first
show, seals swim in the pools
at Sea Life Park's Whaler's Cove on
windward Oahu (above).

ALOHA STADIUM

The Aloha Stadium (left) is located on the outskirts of Honolulu about 17 miles (27 km) from Waikiki Beach. The stadium is host to many varied events including football and baseball matches, rock concerts and the well-known flea market which is popular with tourists.

HONOLULU HIGH-RISE

Modern high-rise buildings, such as Number One Waterfront Plaza (right), now dominate the skyline of Honolulu.

SCIENCE CITY
Science City on the summit of
Haleakala. Lasers fired from these
domes at the eclipsing moon and
other objects in near space have
measured distances and provided
scientists with information useful in
developing the U.S. government's
"Star Wars" defense system.

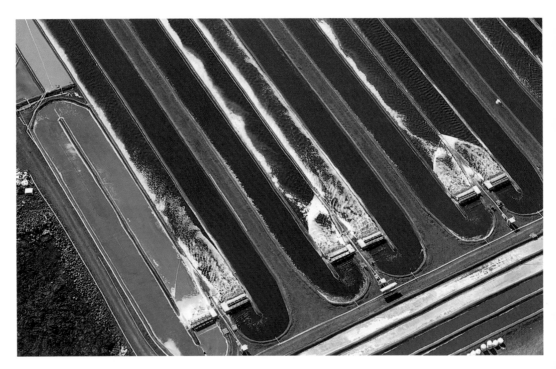

INDUSTRY
AND
AGRICULTURE

For the first half of the twentieth century the Hawaiian economy was dominated by agricultural enterprises, particularly pineapple and sugar plantations. During this time, the business and political arenas were heavily influenced by the "Big Five" corporations, which owned large plantations and other commercial enterprises. The Second World War had a dramatic impact on Hawaiian society and industry. The military presence in the islands was increased, and for the duration of the war Hawaii was placed under martial law. During the post-war years the military was the most significant industry in Hawaii. However, in the late twentieth century tourism became Hawaii's leading industry.

HALAWA BAY
A multi-use jetty (left) built on the point at Halawa Bay on the sparsely populated island of Molokai.

AN INTER-ISLAND BARGE
Loaded with Matson shipping containers and new cars, a Young Brothers inter-island barge heads out of Honolulu Harbor (right). The harbor itself has a reputation for being remarkably clean. Live corals and reef fish can be seen through the clear water near the piers.

AQUACULTURE PONDS

Aeration machines churn the water in the OTEC aquaculture ponds in Kona, Hawaii. Algae of deep green spirulina and orange beta carotene are being developed as food supplements for people who want nutrient-rich diets. Other aquaculture ventures in the islands include shrimp, prawns, oysters and several varieties of fish.

PEARL HARBOR

Part of a mothballed fleet of submarines and destroyers sits in Middle Loch, Pearl Harbor (left), after more than 25 years of service. From right, the submarines ex-USS *Darter* and *Barbel*; and the *Edwards*, *Morten* and another of the Forrest Sherman class of destroyers. In 1987 the ex-USS *Edwards* was taken out of mothballs and used by ABC to film *War and Remembrance*.

THE ARIZONA MEMORIAL

On December 7, 1941, a flurry of torpedoes and bombs dropped from Japanese planes sank the battleship USS *Arizona*. The wreck was beyond salvaging, and the bodies of the 1,100 sailors who went down with her were left in the hold. Rainbow slicks from the ship's leaking fuel tanks still color the water. The white structure straddling the hulk is the Arizona Memorial (right), built in 1962 and designed by the Honolulu architect Alfred Preis.

ON PARADE

The troops salute at Palm Circle, Fort Shafter, Honolulu (left). From World War II until the mid-1980s, when tourism took over, the military was the biggest industry in the islands.

A LIGHTHOUSE ON HAWAII

This Coast Guard "skeletal tower" lighthouse (right) sits inland on Cape Kumukahi, the easternmost point of the "Big Island." In 1960 a flank eruption of Kilauea volcano sent a slow-moving flow of aa (clinker) lava rumbling toward the lighthouse and several nearby houses. University of Hawaii geologists directed bulldozers to throw up rock walls, which held back the flow. The paint on the lighthouse blistered in the heat and fell on the lava, leaving white specks that remain to this day.

OLD WRECKS

A colossal junkyard on the Wailuku plain, Maui (left). Traffic woes and abandoned vehicles have spurred the organization of a movement called ZAG, Zero Automobile Growth, whose proposal for car recycling is simple: "For every car imported to Hawaii, one must be deported."

KALANIANAOLE HIGHWAY

Leaving Honolulu behind, a tour bus heads east along Kalanianaole Highway beneath Koko Crater (right). Koko means "blood," and the name derives from the red dirt in the area or from a legendary fisherman who was bitten by a shark here.

THE WRECKER'S YARD
Old cars and buses await destruction
at a wrecker's yard in the Waianai
Valley on Oahu (left).

ROCK FISHING
A group of people fish off the rocks
near Waikiki Beach (above).

TOURISM

In the 1920s tourism began as a fledgling industry in Hawaii. Now it is the most significant sector of the economy. Each year many thousands of people visit the islands to enjoy the beaches and the surf, the tropical rain forests and spectacular scenery. Tourism and tourists have changed the face of the Hawaiian Islands. Honolulu, the point of arrival for most tourists, has become a large modern city complete with skyscrapers and freeways. Resorts and hotels, theme parks and golf courses have been built in many parts of the islands. The needs of the tourist industry and the increase in the population place the natural resources of the islands under severe pressure.

RENOWNED WAIKIKI BEACH
The crown jewel of Hawaii's resort market (left), the strand most trod upon by movie stars and world leaders, the fundamental Hawaiian vacation experience, perhaps the most famous beach in the world—Waikiki.

WAITING FOR A WAVE
These surfers (right) probably did not have much luck as the surf report for Waikiki Beach this day was "flat to a foot."

HANA HIGHWAY

All these people had the same idea: rent a red car and ride the famous Hana Highway on Maui (left). The journey itself is the destination on this "Highway to Heaven." With more curves per mile than any other roadway on Earth, the drive from Kahului to Hana is a mind-boggling challenge with 617 curves (the ones here are too gradual to count) and 56 bridges.

LUXURIOUS POOLS

About the Hyatt Regency pool on Hawaii (right), one tourist said, "It's so close to the ocean you could throw a seashell into it." Most of Hawaii's vacationers remain poolside—even in Waikiki—because they prefer the safety and comfort of easy access and the proximity of a bar.

HANAUMA BAY

Once a remote, pristine spot Hanauma Bay (left) has become too popular. As many as 13,000 people have crossed its beach in a single day. Every year 2.5 million visitors come, most shuttled in by tour companies operating out of Waikiki, 10 miles (16 km) away. In 1967 the bay became an underwater park, and fishing was banned. By 1990 so many people had come to see and feed the tame fish and had so fouled the place with trash and stirred-up silt that the City and County of Honolulu began to implement access restrictions.

SOUTH KOHALA

A band of asphalt and manicured landscaping slashes through sunset-reddened lava in South Kohala, Hawaii (right).

A SHIFTING SANDBAR
Kaneohe Bay sandbar, a favorite landing for boaters and windsurfers off Oahu. Dry only at the lowest tides, the sands shift with the seasons.

SPECTACULAR VIEWS
Tourists line the rails at a lookout
above Waimea Canyon, Kauai (left).

WAILUA RIVERBOATS
Tourist boats (right) cruise along the
idyllic Wailua River, which leads to
the spectacular Wailua Falls, on Kauai.
This island has the only navigable rivers
in Hawaii.

HONOLULU ZOO
A group of flamingos at the Honolulu Zoo (left), which is located between Waikiki Beach and Diamond Head.

LEI DAY
Celebrating Lei Day at Queen Kapiolani Park in Honolulu (right). Lei Day is held every year on the first of May. The festivities include a lei contest and highlight traditional Hawaiian arts and crafts.

TOURIST CRUISE

A group of tourists (left) enjoy the sunshine and sea on a trip aboard the *Sheraton Rainbow* off Waikiki Beach.

SURFBOARD RIDERS

Two surfers (right) on long boards paddle in search of the perfect wave.

KONA VILLAGE RESORT

For travelers seeking seclusion and simplicity, the Kona Village Resort on the "Big Island" (left) offers "plush primitive" thatched bungalows that look weathered and rustic outside but inside feature typical hotel amenities: carpeting, tubs and showers, and ceiling fans. In the bay, tame fish and manta rays swim right up to snorkelers' masks.

KALII WAI RIVER

Kalii Wai River settles into Kalihi Wai Bay (right) on the north shore of Kauai. Looking like a small version of Waimea on Oahu, the river here will swell during the rainy season and cut a gully through the beach sand.

THE "SHAKA" SIGN

A group of Japanese tourists on a raft in Maunalua Bay, Oahu (above). Locals give "shaka" signs. This greeting began in the 1950s in imitation of a Laie man who was missing three fingers on one hand. He waved with the thumb and little finger sticking out, and when he waved he said, "Shaka, brah!"

A WEDDING IN HAWAII

A beachfront church in the Honolulu suburb of Aina Haina (right) has become a popular spot for Japanese weddings. Tour companies in Japan offer engaged couples travel packages that include a videotaped exchange of vows in Paradise.

HONOLULU HARBOR

The SS *Independence* inter-island cruise ship and the Aloha Tower (left). Built in 1926 to control maritime traffic in Honolulu Harbor, the 10-story Aloha Tower was for 30 years the tallest building in Hawaii.

IDEAL FOR WATERSPORTS

A windsurfer enjoys the good conditions off Diamond Head, Oahu (right). Windsurfing is just one of the many watersports for which the area around Waikiki Beach and Diamond Head is suitable.

A WELL-EARNED VIEW
A group of tourists enjoy the view after hiking to the lookout atop Diamond Head (left). The summit is 760 feet (235 m) above sea level and offers a magnificent view over Waikiki Beach and Honolulu.

MUANA LUA BAY
Jet skiers at play on Muana Lua Bay on Oahu (right).

AN AFTERNOON CRUISE
Pausing to wave and flash "shaka" signs, these Honolulu sailors enjoy a nautical lunch (above). There are about 700 yachts moored at the Ala Wai Small Boat Harbor in Waikiki.

HYATT REGENCY RESORT
A collection of geometric shapes arranged along the "Big Island's" rugged Kohala coast: the Hyatt Regency resort at Waikoloa (right).

INDEX

Entries in *italics* indicate illustrations and photos.

INDEX continued

ACKNOWLEDGMENTS

Weldon Owen would like to thank the following people: Lisa Boehm, Trudie Craig, Peta Gorman, Michael Hann, Puddingburn Publishing Services (index)
TEXT Steven Goldsberry
MAP Stuart McVicar
PHOTOGRAPHS Reg Morrison, Corel Corporation